Preparing to Teach
in the Lifelong Learning Sector:
The New Award

Fifth edition

Preparing to Teach
in the Lifelong Learning Sector:
The New Award
Fifth edition

Ann Gravells

Los Angeles | London | New Delhi
Singapore | Washington DC

Learning Matters
An imprint of SAGE Publications Ltd
1 Oliver's Yard
55 City Road
London EC1Y 1SP

SAGE Publications Inc.
2455 Teller Road
Thousand Oaks, California 91320

SAGE Publications India Pvt Ltd
B 1/I 1 Mohan Cooperative Industrial Area
Mathura Road
New Delhi 110 044

SAGE Publications Asia-Pacific Pte Ltd
3 Church Street
#10-04 Samsung Hub
Singapore 049483

Editor: Amy Thornton
Development editor: Jennifer Clark
Production controller: Chris Marke
Production management: Deer Park Productions
Marketing manager: Zoe Seaton
Cover design: Toucan Designs
Typeset by: PDQ Typesetting, Newcastle-under-Lyme
Printed by: TJ International Ltd, Padstow, Cornwall

First published as 'Delivering Adult Learning' in 2006
Reprinted with amendments 2006
Second edition 2007
Reprinted 2000 (three times)
Third edition 2008
Reprinted 2008 (three times)
Reprinted 2009 (three times)
Fourth edition 2011
Reprinted 2011 (twice)
Fifth edition 2012

Library of Congress Control Number 2011944212

British Library Cataloguing in Publication data

A catalogue record for this book is available from the British Library

ISBN 978 0 85725 773 4

CONTENTS

I would like to thank the following for their support and contributions while working on the new edition of this book: Peter Adeney, Angela Faulkener, John Fewings, Gaynor Mount, Susan Simpson and Jacklyn Williams.

I would also like to thank my father Bob Gravells for his excellent proof reading skills – even though he knew nothing about teacher training when he started, he certainly does now; also, my husband Peter Frankish, who never complains about the amount of time I spend in the office and makes me endless cups of tea to keep me going; and Jennifer Clark, and Amy Thornton from Learning Matters, who are always at the end of the phone when I feel under pressure and need motivation and encouragement.

Thanks also go to the staff and students of the teacher training department at Bishop Burton College, who always inspire me.

I would also like to thank readers of previous editions of this book who have given valuable feedback which has greatly assisted me when preparing the new edition.

Every effort has been made to trace the copyright holders and to obtain their permission for the use of copyright material. The publisher and author will gladly receive any information enabling them to rectify any error or omission in subsequent editions.

Ann Gravells
January 2012
www.anngravells.co.uk

Ann Gravells is a lecturer in teacher training at Bishop Burton College in East Yorkshire and a consultant to the University of Cambridge's Institute of Continuing Education's Assessment Network. She has been teaching since 1983.

She is an external quality consultant for the City & Guilds teacher training qualifications, a presenter of events and a consultant for various other projects.

Ann is a director of her own company, Ann Gravells Ltd, an educational consultancy which specialises in teaching, training and quality assurance. She delivers events and courses nationwide.

Ann holds a Masters in Educational Management, a PGCE, a Degree in Education, and a City & Guilds Medal of Excellence for teaching. Ann is a Fellow of the Institute for Learning and holds QTLS status.

She is often asked how her surname should be pronounced. The 'vells' part of Gravells is pronounced like 'bells'.

Ann is the author of:

- *Achieving your TAQA Assessor and Internal Quality Assurer Award*
- *Delivering Employability Skills in the Lifelong Learning Sector*
- *Passing PTLLS Assessments*
- *Preparing to Teach in the Lifelong Learning Sector*
- *Principles and Practice of Assessment in the Lifelong Learning Sector*
- *What is Teaching in the Lifelong Learning Sector?*

co-author of:

- *Equality and Diversity in the Lifelong Learning Sector*
- *Passing CTLLS Assessments*
- *Planning and Enabling Learning in the Lifelong Learning Sector*

and Ann has edited:

- *Study Skills for PTLLS*

The author welcomes any comments from readers; please contact her via her website: www.anngravells.co.uk.

In this chapter you will learn about:

- the structure of the book and how to use it
- the PTLLS Award
- Qualifications and Credit Framework (QCF)
- teaching in the Lifelong Learning Sector
- Lifelong Learning professional teaching standards
- The Institute for Learning (IfL)

The structure of the book and how to use it

Congratulations upon making the decision to become a teacher in the Lifelong Learning Sector. You might be working towards a teaching qualification or just want to find out what it's like to be a teacher. This book will give you the information you need to set you on your learning journey. It has been written with new teachers in mind, in a language which is not full of educational jargon. This book will act as a good introduction to teaching in the Lifelong Learning Sector; however, you may also wish to refer to the websites and texts listed at the end of each chapter to inform your learning further.

The book is structured in chapters which relate to the full process of teaching and learning often referred to as the training cycle or teaching and learning cycle. The chapters cover the content of the four units of the PTLLS Award at level 3 and level 4. The book is also applicable to anyone working towards the Learning and Development qualifications.

The content of PTLLS is the same at both level 3 and level 4; the difference in level is expressed in the amount of work you will be required to submit. For example, if you are taking level 3, you will *explain* how or why you do something; at level 4 you will *analyse* how or why you do it. If you are working towards level 4, you will need to carry out relevant research, reference your work to theorists, use an academic style of writing and refer to other texts in addition to this. At least three out of the four units must be achieved at level 4 (i.e. one unit can be at level 3). Further information and guidance regarding academic writing and research are available in the companion book *Study Skills for PTLLS* by Jacklyn Williams.

You can work logically through the book by starting with Chapter I or you can just look up appropriate topics in the index to access aspects relevant to your current study. There are activities to enable you to think about how you teach, examples to help you understand the process of teaching and learning and extension activities to develop, stretch and challenge your learning further. While this book covers the theory required for the PTLLS Award, the companion book *Passing PTLLS Assessments* by Ann Gravells will help you put theory into practice and structure your evidence to meet the learning outcomes.

Each chapter is cross-referenced to the overarching *Professional Standards for Teachers, Tutors and Trainers in the Lifelong Learning Sector* and the individual PTLLS units. Throughout this book, the generic term *teacher* is used, even though you might be called something different: for example, *assessor, facilitator, instructor, lecturer, coach, counsellor, trainer* or *tutor*. The generic term *student* is also used and refers to other terms such as *apprentice, candidate, learner, participant, pupil* or *trainee* however the term learner is used for qualifications which are on the Qualifications and Credit Framework.

If you are teaching nationally or internationally, some of the regulations and organisations referred to in the book may only be relevant in England. You are therefore advised to check what is current and applicable to the nation or country in which you work.

The appendices contain the PTLLS Award learning outcomes and assessment criteria at level 3 and level 4. There is also a useful teaching and learning checklist.

The PTLLS Award

The PTLLS Award contains four units which are available at level 3 or level 4. Each is 3 credits on the QCF. To achieve the PTLLS Award, you need a total of 12 credits which equates to 120 hours of learning. This will consist of approximately 48 hours' contact with a teacher such as attending sessions and being assessed. You will have approximately 72 hours of non-contact time which will be for reading, research, completing assignments and gathering evidence towards the units. The chapters in this book are cross referenced to the four units.

PTLLS is made up of the following four units at level 3 and 4, each with 3 credits, or their accepted alternatives:

- Roles, responsibilities and relationships in lifelong learning
- Understanding inclusive learning and teaching in lifelong learning
- Using inclusive learning and teaching approaches in lifelong learning
- Principles of assessment in lifelong learning.

Accepted alternatives come from the Learning and Development qualification. However, you will need to check with your assessor which ones can be used as there are rules regarding which units can be combined to make the PTLLS Award. For example, if you have already achieved the unit *Understanding the principles and practices of assessment* you could use it as an alternative to *Principles of assessment in lifelong learning*. The content of the following Learning and Development units is covered within the chapters of this book, although not directly cross-referenced.

The accepted alternative units are:

- Facilitate learning and development for individuals (level 3, 6 credits)
- Facilitate learning and development in groups (level 3, 6 credits)
- Manage learning and development in groups (level 4, 6 credits)
- Understanding the principles and practices of assessment (level 3, 3 credits).

If you have achieved any of the accepted equivalents prior to taking the PTLLS Award, they will be classed as Recognition of Prior Learning (RPL) which exempts you from retaking them. You should have been given a Unique Learner Number (ULN) when you achieved the unit and this number will automatically recognise your achievement through the QCF. You will need to produce your certificate if asked to by your assessor.

All qualifications on the QCF use the terms *learning outcomes* and *assessment criteria*. The learning outcomes state what the learner *will do*, and the assessment criteria what the learner *can do*. You can see these for the four main units of the PTLLS Award in the appendices. Units are usually *knowledge based* (to assess understanding) or *performance based* (to assess competence).

This book covers all the requirements of the learning outcomes and assessment criteria to help you achieve the PTLLS Award. However, you are responsible for keeping up to date with the subject that you will teach. While the book will help you with ideas for teaching and assessing, you will need to adapt these to suit your specialist subject. You also need to ensure your own literacy, language, numeracy, and information and communication technology (ICT) skills are of a good quality and to at least level 2 on the QCF.

Qualifications and Credit Framework

The QCF (SCQF in Scotland) is a system for recognising skills and qualifications by awarding credit values to units. A credit value of 1 equates to 10 learning hours. These credit values enable you to see how long it would take an average student to achieve a unit. For example, the *Roles, responsibilities and relationships in lifelong learning* unit is 3 credits which equates to 30 hours. The total hours include *contact time* with a teacher and assessor, and *non-contact time* for individual study and assignment work.

There are three sizes of qualifications with titles and associated credit values:

- Award (1 to 12 credits)
- Certificate (13 to 36 credits)
- Diploma (37 credits or more).

The terms Award, Certificate and Diploma do not relate to progression, i.e. you don't start with an Award, progress to the Certificate and then the Diploma. The terms relate to how big the qualification is (i.e. its size) which is based on the total number of credits. For example, a Diploma with 37 credits would equate to 370 hours of learning and is therefore a bigger qualification than an Award with 12 credits and 120 hours.

The difficulty of the qualification is defined by its level. The QCF has 9 levels; entry level plus 1 to 8 (there are 12 levels in Scotland).

A rough comparison of the levels to existing qualifications is:

1 – GCSEs (grades D–G)
2 – GCSEs (grade A*–C)
3 – Advanced level (A level)
4 – Vocational Qualification level 4, Higher National Certificate (HNC)
5 – Vocational Qualification level 5, Degree, Higher National Diploma (HND)
6 – Honours degree
7 – Masters degree
8 – Doctor of Philosophy (PhD).

Teaching in the Lifelong Learning Sector

Teaching is about helping someone reach their full potential, whether this is for personal or professional reasons. The Lifelong Learning Sector can include students from age 14 upwards, therefore you have the opportunity to help make a difference to someone's life and career, which can be very rewarding. If you are new to teaching, this could be because you are contemplating a change of profession or you are required to take a particular teaching qualification because of your job role. Perhaps you have a hobby or a trade you would like to teach others; you know you are good at it and feel you have the experience and knowledge which you could pass on to others. While this book will guide you through the process of teaching and learning, it is up to you to ensure you are current with your subject knowledge. Depending upon where and what you are going to teach, you may not need to be qualified in your particular subject, but be able to demonstrate appropriate experience and knowledge at a particular level.

The most important aspect of teaching is to ensure that learning is taking place. If you are currently teaching, your delivery methods might be based on experiences of how you were taught in the past. However, there are many teaching and learning approaches you could use and this book will hopefully give you new ideas to teach in a more professional, engaging and inclusive manner. Teaching isn't just about delivering to groups in a classroom; it can take place in many different environments such as the workplace, public, private or voluntary settings, outdoors, or online via the internet.

Lifelong Learning professional teaching standards

In September 2007, standards came into effect for all new teachers in the Lifelong Learning Sector who teach on government-funded programmes in England. This includes all post-16 education, including further education, adult and community learning, work-based learning and offender education. Please see the web links at the end of the chapter for Northern Ireland, Scotland and Wales.

The key purpose of the teacher is to create effective and stimulating opportunities for learning through high-quality teaching that enables the development and progression of all students. Teachers in the Lifelong Learning Sector should value all students individually and equally. They are committed to lifelong learning and professional development and strive for continuous improvement through reflective practice.

The full standards encompass six domains:

A Professional values and practice

B Learning and teaching

C Specialist learning and teaching

D Planning for learning

E Assessment for learning

F Access and progression.

The chapters in this book are cross-referenced to these domains; however, the standards are incorporated into the following qualifications:

- Preparing to Teach in the Lifelong Learning Sector (PTLLS)
- Certificate in Teaching in the Lifelong Learning Sector (CTLLS)
- Diploma in Teaching in the Lifelong Learning Sector (DTLLS).

All new teachers must undertake the PTLLS Award at the beginning of their career. This can be as a discrete Award or embedded in the Certificate or Diploma. Higher education institutions can still use the terms *Certificate in Education* and *Postgraduate* or *Professional Certificate in Education*. However, the content is the same as the Diploma, but it may be offered at a higher level. See Chapter 7 for details regarding progression from PTLLS, as the next qualification you take (either CTLLS or DTLLS) is dependent solely upon your job role as a teacher.

As you progress through the teaching qualifications, you will need to meet all the relevant criteria relating to the scope, knowledge and practice required in your job role (referenced by: **S** for **S**cope, **K** for **K**nowledge or **P** for **P**ractice at the end of each chapter). You should have a mentor, someone in the same subject as yourself who can help and support you.

The qualifications have been developed based upon the QCF model which has mandatory and optional units at different levels with different credit values. The units and credits can be built up to form relevant qualifications over time. The teaching qualifications start at level 3 on the QCF and can be obtained through an Awarding Organisation (AO) or Higher Education Institute (HEI).

The Institute for Learning

The Institute for Learning (IfL) is the professional body for teachers, trainers, tutors and trainee teachers in the Learning and Skills Sector. Teachers should register with the IfL and follow a Code of Professional Practice (2008) along with the associated disciplinary processes. If you haven't already done so, you will need to register with the IfL via their website, www.ifl.ac.uk.

While working towards your PTLLS Award, it would be extremely beneficial for you to have a mentor, someone who can help and support you, not only with teaching skills, but also with your specialist subject. Your mentor could observe you teaching and give you developmental feedback; conversely, you could observe them to gain useful ideas and tips for teaching and learning.

Summary

In this chapter you have learnt about:

- the structure of the book and how to use it
- the PTLLS Award
- Qualifications and Credit Framework
- teaching in the Lifelong Learning Sector
- Lifelong Learning professional teaching standards
- the Institute for Learning.

Theory focus
References and further information

Gravells, A (2012) *Passing PTLLS Assessments*. Exeter: Learning Matters.

Gravells, A (2012) *What is Teaching in the Lifelong Learning Sector?* Exeter: Learning Matters.

IfL (2008) *Code of Professional Practice: Raising concerns about IfL members*. London: Institute for Learning.

LLUK (2006) *New Overarching Professional Standards for Teachers, Tutors and Trainers in the Lifelong Learning Sector*. London: LLUK.

Williams, J (2012) *Study Skills for PTLLS*. Exeter: Learning Matters.

Websites

Ann Gravells (information regarding teaching qualifications)
   – www.anngravells.co.uk

Further Education Teachers' Qualifications (England) Regulations (2007)
   – www. legislation.gov.uk/uksi/2007/2264/contents/made

Further Education Teachers' Qualifications (Wales) – http://tiny.cc/ol0oc

Institute for Learning – www.ifl.ac.uk

Learning and Skills Improvement Service – www.lsis.org.uk

Ofqual – www.ofqual.gov.uk

Post Compulsory Education and Training Network – www.pcet.net

Professional Standards for Lecturers in Scotland's Colleges –
http://tiny.cc/3w9jg

Qualifications and Credit Framework – http://tinyurl.com/447bgy2

Teaching Qualifications for Northern Ireland – http://tiny.cc/2bexb

Scottish Credit and Qualifications Framework – www.scqf.org.uk

1 TEACHING AND LEARNING

Introduction

In this chapter you will learn about:

- roles and responsibilities of a teacher
- boundaries of teaching
- record keeping
- legislation and codes of practice

There are activities and examples to help you reflect on the above which will assist your understanding of the process of teaching and learning. At the end of each section there are extension activities to stretch and challenge your learning further.

At the end of the chapter is a cross-referencing grid showing how the chapter's contents contribute towards the professional teaching standards and PTLLS units.

Roles and responsibilities of a teacher

Most careers are quite challenging and demanding, and teaching is no exception to this. However, it can be very rewarding when you see your students' achievements and success, which is a direct result of your contribution. Your main role as a teacher should be to teach your subject in a way that actively involves and engages your students during every session. However, it's not just about teaching, it's also about the learning that takes place as a result. You should use clear language at an appropriate level and in terms your students will understand, motivating them to want to learn more. You should also manage the learning process from when your students commence to when they complete, ensuring you assess their progress, give relevant feedback and keep appropriate records.

How you do this will depend upon your subject, the age and experience of your students and the environment you will teach in. Becoming a good teacher includes being enthusiastic and passionate about your subject, being approachable and taking pride in your work, which will all be conveyed to your students through your teaching approaches.

Example

Zak always arrives early to his sessions, he ensures the room is tidy and organises the tables and chairs in a way that encourages communication. He creates an approachable environment and delivers his subject with passion and enthusiasm. He uses lots of examples and anecdotes to relate his subject to real life. He includes all his learners by addressing them personally, yet remains fair with the support and advice he gives. He always tidies up afterwards and e-mails additional learning materials as required. His learners see how conscientious and professional Zak is and begin to emulate this by being early, being polite and submitting work on time.

A good first impression will help establish a positive working relationship with your students. The way you dress, act, respond to questions, offer support, etc., will also influence your students. They don't need to know anything personal about you, but they will probably make assumptions about you. If asked personal questions, try not to give out any information: by remaining a professional, and not becoming too friendly, you will retain their respect. Most teachers are on first name terms with their students. However, you will need to decide what is appropriate to your situation. Establishing routines will help your sessions flow smoothly; for example, always starting on time, setting and keeping to time limits for activities and breaks, and finishing on time.

Activity

How could you create a good first impression with your students? What would influence this, for example your own previous experiences of attending a session?

The teaching and learning cycle

The teaching and learning cycle is so called as it can start at any stage and keep on going. However, all stages must be addressed for teaching and learning to be effective. The chapters in this book are based on the cycle, which consists of the stages outlined in Figure I.I below.

Figure I.I The teaching and learning cycle

Your role will usually follow the cycle and briefly involve:

- identifying needs – finding out what your organisation's, your own, and potential students' needs are, carrying out initial assessments, agreeing individual learning plans

- planning learning – preparing a scheme of work, session plans and teaching and learning materials to ensure you cover the requirements of the syllabus, liaising with others

- facilitating learning – teaching and facilitating learning using a variety of approaches

- assessing learning – checking your students have gained the necessary skills and knowledge

- quality assurance and evaluation – obtaining feedback from others, evaluating yourself and the programme in order to make improvements for the future. Evaluation should also be an ongoing process throughout all stages of the cycle.

Most teachers follow the cycle from beginning to end; however, your job role might not require you to be involved with all aspects. You will probably undertake a variety of roles during your teaching career, each having various responsibilities or duties that you must carry out. The job roles do not relate to whether you are employed full-time or part-time, but to the duties you will perform. There are two teaching roles in the further education sector in England:

- Associate teaching role which has fewer teaching responsibilities and will be performed by those who are expected to gain the status of Associate Teacher, Learning and Skills (ATLS). An Associate Teacher will usually teach using materials prepared by others.

- Full teaching role which represents the full range of responsibilities performed by those who are expected to gain the status of Qualified Teacher, Learning and Skills (QTLS). A Full Teacher will perform all aspects of the teaching and learning cycle.

Table 1.1 on page 12 lists examples of teaching roles and responsibilities, based on the teaching and learning cycle. Don't be concerned by the amount of detail in the table; your job role might not require you to carry them all out. If there is anything you are unsure of at the moment, as you progress through the book it should all become clear.

To teach effectively involves not only the approaches you use to teach your subject, but many other factors that go before and after the taught session. This

Table 1.1 Examples of teaching roles and responsibilities

Roles	Responsibilities
Identifying needs	
• arranging for suitable initial assessments to take place; for example, to ascertain current skills and knowledge • carrying out interviews with students • identifying any barriers or challenges to learning • identifying any particular student, self and organisational needs • identifying learning styles • knowing the boundaries within which to work • participating in recruitment activities	• attending promotional events to publicise the programme • dressing appropriately • ensuring students are on the right programme • following organisational policies and procedures • giving appropriate information, advice and guidance • helping students arrange funding/grants • keeping records of what was discussed and agreed • maintaining confidentiality • referring students to other people or agencies when necessary • registering with the IfL • undertaking a Criminal Records Bureau (CRB) check
Planning learning	
• communicating appropriately and effectively with other professionals • planning what will be taught and when • preparing teaching and learning resources and activities	• agreeing individual learning plans • carrying out risk assessments • creating a safe, positive and accessible learning environment for students and visitors • designing a scheme of work, session plans and appropriate materials and resources • having a contingency plan in place • liaising with others • obtaining the relevant syllabus or qualification handbook • writing realistic aims
Facilitating learning	
• carrying out tutorial reviews • communicating appropriately and effectively with students • conforming to professional codes of practice and values • embedding language, literacy, numeracy and ICT • establishing ground rules • following awarding organisation and external body requirements • inducting students to the organisation and programme • maintaining a safe and supportive learning environment • promoting appropriate behaviour and respect • promoting equality and valuing diversity • teaching in an inclusive and engaging way	• acting and speaking appropriately • acting professionally and with integrity • being qualified/experienced to teach your subject • carrying out administrative requirements • completing attendance records • dealing with behaviour issues as they occur • differentiating teaching and learning materials and approaches • engaging and encouraging learning • following health and safety safeguarding requirements and relevant legislation and codes of practice • knowing who the appointed first aider is

Facilitating learning *continued*	
<ul><li>using a variety of teaching and learning approaches to motivate students</li><li>using icebreakers and energisers effectively</li></ul>	<ul><li>following professional values and ethics</li><li>following up absences</li><li>helping and supporting students as appropriate</li><li>incorporating new technology</li><li>keeping records of what has been taught and to whom</li><li>keeping up to date with developments relating to your subject</li><li>maintaining a professional relationship with students</li><li>not forcing your own attitudes, values and beliefs upon your students</li><li>tidying the area after each session</li><li>using appropriate equipment and resources</li><li>using appropriate teaching and learning approaches</li></ul>
Assessing learning	
<ul><li>assessing progress</li><li>following awarding organisation and external body requirements</li></ul>	<ul><li>assessing work within an agreed time period</li><li>checking for plagiarism if applicable</li><li>ensuring decisions are valid, reliable, fair and ethical</li><li>giving feedback to students</li><li>informing students of their right to appeal</li><li>keeping records of individual achievements</li><li>maintaining confidentiality</li><li>preparing realistic assessment materials</li><li>standardising decisions with others</li><li>using a variety of assessment methods: initial, formative, summative, formal and informal</li></ul>
Quality assurance and Evaluation	
<ul><li>evaluating how well the programme was planned and delivered</li><li>improving the teaching and learning process</li></ul>	<ul><li>attending meetings</li><li>encouraging student development and progression</li><li>encouraging ongoing feedback from students and others</li><li>evaluating each session you taught, along with the teaching and learning approaches and materials used</li><li>helping students achieve their full potential</li><li>liaising with others, e.g. external verifiers and inspectors</li><li>maintaining own professional development and subject currency</li><li>partaking in organisational quality assurance processes</li><li>standardising practice with others</li></ul>

includes planning your sessions, preparing your teaching materials, assessing your students, marking work, giving feedback and evaluating yourself and the experience your students have. Never underestimate the amount of time you will need to dedicate to the role.

Your personality and mannerisms will be noticed by your students. You may do things you are not aware of; for example, waving your arms around or fidgeting. It is really useful to make a visual recording of one of your sessions to enable you to watch yourself afterwards. You may see things you didn't realise you did or things that you would like to change. Smiling when you meet your students will help you and them relax.

If you are new to teaching, you may find you are teaching in the same way you were taught at school or college. This could be lecturing, reading from a book or writing information on a board, which might not have been very effective for you. You won't yet know all the other methods you could use to make learning interesting and engaging. Active learning helps people remember; passive learning may lead them to forget. As you become more experienced at teaching, your confidence will grow and you will be able to experiment with different approaches, as not all teaching methods suit all students.

Extension Activity

Think about the subject you would like to teach, the age group of your students and the environment in which you will teach. What do you consider your roles and responsibilities will be to ensure learning is effective? If you are currently teaching, compare your responses with your job description.

Boundaries of teaching

You will have professional boundaries within which to work and it's important not to overstep these by becoming too personal with your students. Boundaries are about knowing where your role as a teacher stops and working within the limits of that role. Table 1.2 on page 15 lists some of the boundaries you may encounter in relation to the teaching and learning cycle.

Example

Navinda had been teaching a group of 16 students once a week for six weeks. She occasionally e-mailed them between sessions to inform them of room changes. Two of her students sent her an e-mail inviting her to join their social networking site. She politely refused, to ensure that she remained professional in her role as their teacher.

Table 1.2 Boundaries of teaching

Identifying needs	<ul><li>demands from managers</li><li>expectations of students</li><li>funding constraints</li><li>knowing what advice and/or information can and cannot be given to students</li><li>lack of information regarding students' requirements</li><li>students not at the required starting level</li><li>negative culture within a department or organisation</li><li>organisational policies, procedures and administrative requirements</li><li>requirements of codes of practice, awarding organisations and external bodies</li><li>standards and levels students are expected to achieve</li></ul>
Planning learning	<ul><li>capability of students to achieve</li><li>equality and diversity policies</li><li>financial concerns – organisation and students</li><li>health and safety regulations</li><li>lack of access to computers and technology-based learning materials</li><li>lack of adequate equipment and access to resources, e.g. photocopying</li><li>not enough knowledge of individual students and their learning styles</li><li>requirements of, or a lack of understanding of the syllabus or qualification requirements</li><li>unsupportive colleagues</li></ul>
Facilitating learning	<ul><li>ability of students, e.g. lack of English</li><li>barriers to learning such as access, or lack of specialist equipment and resources</li><li>behaviour issues</li><li>broken or faulty equipment and resources</li><li>changes in legislation, codes of practice, policies and procedures</li><li>deadlines and targets</li><li>disruptive students</li><li>inability to be flexible when teaching, to take into account needs of students</li><li>inappropriate actions of self or students</li><li>inappropriate seating or working areas</li><li>lack of a suitable environment and/or resources</li><li>lack of own subject knowledge</li><li>students' lack of motivation, demands or high expectations</li><li>students' personal and welfare issues</li><li>not enough time for teaching and student support</li><li>not hindering an individual's progress just because they are learning more quickly than the group</li><li>own personal problems</li><li>requirements of relevant legislation, e.g. risk assessments</li><li>safeguarding requirements</li></ul>
Assessing learning	<ul><li>data protection and confidentiality</li><li>demands of paperwork and administration</li><li>meeting deadlines and targets</li><li>not being biased or unfair with judgements</li><li>not enough evidence from students to make a decision</li><li>not giving some students more support than others</li><li>not passing students just to achieve your targets</li><li>objectivity when making decisions</li></ul>
Quality assurance and Evaluation	<ul><li>awarding organisation's demands, e.g. internal and external verification</li><li>lack of time to attend training events, standardisation activities, continuing professional development (CPD) or meetings</li><li>organisation's targets and demands</li><li>own ability to listen to and react to feedback</li></ul>

You need to remain in control, be fair and ethical with all your students and not demonstrate any favouritism towards particular students; for example, by giving one more support than the others. You might feel it sensible to make a telephone call to a student who has been absent but making regular calls would be inappropriate. Giving your personal telephone number to students could be seen as encouraging informal contact, and you may get calls or texts which are not suitable or relevant. You might not want to take your break with your students or join their social networking sites as you could become more of a friend than a teacher. It is unprofessional to use bad language, to touch students in an inappropriate way or to let your personal problems affect your work. Boundaries also include the constraints you might be under as a teacher; for example, the amount of paperwork you are expected to complete or the lack of funding or resources. Boundaries can often be interpreted as the negative aspects to your roles and responsibilities.

Professional relationships and responsibilities to others

Your main responsibility will be to your students; however, there will be other professionals with whom you will need to liaise at some point. These could include other teachers, technicians, support workers, administration staff and caretakers within the organisation. You might also need to liaise with those external to your organisation such as parents, guardians, employers, inspectors and visitors. You should always remain professional when in contact with others and not overstep the boundary of your role.

Example

Sarah was due to teach a First Aid session and arrived early to set up the room. She found the computer worked but the projector didn't and she had wanted to show a video clip. Instead of calling the computer technician, she moved the equipment to check the cables were connected. In doing so, she accidentally broke the internet cable. Had she not overstepped the boundary of her role and called the technician instead, she would not have caused further problems.

If you are ever in doubt about the boundaries of your role, always ask someone else at your organisation. Never feel you have to do everything yourself in case further problems occur. You might have other roles to undertake such as attending meetings or promotional events. Always remember you are representing your organisation and must act professionally at all times.

What boundaries do you think you will encounter as a teacher and why? How can you effectively overcome them and who would you go to for support and advice?

Record keeping

Records must be maintained, not only to support the teaching and learning process, but to satisfy auditors, inspectors, regulators, verifiers, internal and external quality assurers and your own organisation's requirements. For example, information and data gathering can inform quality assurance, equality and diversity, and health and safety policies. The information contained in records helps to measure learning and the effectiveness and appropriateness of the programme overall. Information such as attendance, progress and achievement could be shared with your colleagues if they are also teaching your students; for example, to look for patterns of attendance or behaviour issues. If accurate records are not maintained, your students' progress may become unstructured and their achievement may not be recognised or documented.

Records must be up to date, accurate, factual and legible whether they are stored manually or electronically. All records should show an audit trail, i.e. track student progress from when they commenced through to their completion. If you happen to be absent for any reason, a colleague will be able to effectively take over if they have access to your records. Data are also useful to your organisation for purposes such as accidents, appeals, equal opportunities and funding purposes.

Example

Nick has set up a file which contains all the documentation relevant to deliver and assess the Certificate in Sport and Recreation. This includes a hard copy of the syllabus, scheme of work, session plans, and teaching and learning materials. He also has a file which contains alphabetical records relating to each of his students. This includes application forms, interview notes, initial assessment results, action plans, tutorial review records and assessment results. These files ensure he has everything to hand, not only to carry out his role effectively, but also for auditors, inspectors and verifiers.

Try and keep on top of your paperwork, even if this is carried out electronically. If you leave it for a while, you may forget to note, sign or date important details. The most important record wll be the register or record of attendance. You need to know who is in your session not only for fire regulations but also to keep track of attendance patterns. If a student is absent regularly you

Table 1.3 Records

Identifying needs	• application forms • diagnostic test results • enrolment forms • initial assessment results • interview notes • student contract • learning style results • learning support records • personal details of students, e.g. address, contacts, disabilities • syllabus or qualification handbook • targets and funding data • ULNs
Planning learning	• individual learning plans/action plans • risk assessments • scheme of work • session plans • timetables
Facilitating learning	• accident/incident forms • agreed ground rules • attendance records/registers • details of student progress and behaviour • disciplinary records • evidence of embedding equality and diversity, language, literacy, numeracy and ICT • induction records • records of what was taught • tutorial review records
Assessing learning	• achievement and success data • assessment plans • audio/digital/video recordings with students • awarding organisation registration numbers • feedback records and decisions/grades (initial, formative and summative) • receipts for the submission and return of assignments • tracking sheets • see *Chapter 6 for a full list of assessment records*
Quality assurance and Evaluation	• complaints and appeals • CPD records • equal opportunities data • inspection reports • internal and external verification and quality assurance reports • minutes of meetings • questionnaire and feedback analysis • registration and certification data • retention and achievement data • standardisation records

should find out why in case they need support. Another important record if you are not employed permanently will be your pay claim. It might not be automatic that you will be paid unless you complete a form.

Records should be kept confidential and secure at your organisation; for example, in a locked filing cabinet. The Data Protection Act (2003) is mandatory for all organisations that hold or process personal data. It contains eight principles, to ensure that data are:

- processed fairly and lawfully
- obtained and used only for specified and lawful purposes
- adequate, relevant and not excessive
- accurate and, where necessary, kept up to date
- kept for no longer than necessary
- processed in accordance with the individual's rights
- kept secure
- transferred only to countries that offer adequate protection.

Table 1.3 on page 18 lists some of the records you might keep, in relation to the teaching and learning cycle.

Extension Activity

Make a list of the records you should maintain and explain why you need to keep them. If you are currently teaching, find out from your mentor what the exact requirements of your organisation are and where and for how long you should keep records.

Legislation and codes of practice

It is important for you to keep up to date with all relevant legislation and codes of practice to ensure you are remaining current with your knowledge and skills, and with any changes or updates that have taken place. These can be grouped into generic, i.e. relating to your role as a teacher, and specific, i.e. relating to your specialist subject.

Generic

These will differ depending upon the context and environment within which you teach. You need to be aware of the requirements of external bodies and regulators such as Ofsted (in England) who inspect provision, along with awarding organisations who will quality-assure their qualifications, and funding agencies who will need data and statistics. Your own organisation will have relevant codes of practice such as disciplinary, conduct, dress, timekeeping and sustainability. There will also be policies and procedures to follow such as appeals, complaints, and risk assessments, etc. If you are employed, you will have received a contract of employment and employee handbook which should state your organisation's rules and procedures.

The following information was current at the time of writing; however, you are advised to check for any changes or updates, and whether they are applicable outside England.

Examples of generic legislation and codes of practice are as follows.

- Children Act (2004): Every Child Matters provided the legal underpinning for the Every Child Matters: Change for Children programme and is covered in more detail in Chapter 5. 'Well-being' is the term used in the Act to define the five Every Child Matters outcomes, which are:
  - be healthy
  - stay safe
  - enjoy and achieve
  - make a positive contribution
  - achieve economic well-being.

- Code of Professional Practice (2008) introduced by the IfL to cover the activities of teachers in the Lifelong Learning Sector. The Code is based on seven behaviours, namely:
  - professional integrity
  - respect
  - reasonable care
  - professional practice
  - criminal offence disclosure
  - responsibility during Institute investigations
  - responsibility.

- Copyright Designs and Patents Act (1988) relates to the copying, adapting and distributing of materials, which includes computer programs and materials found via the internet. Your organisation may have a licence to enable you to photocopy small amounts from books or journals. Anything you do copy should be acknowledged.

- Data Protection Act (2003) made provision for the regulation of the processing of information relating to individuals, including the obtaining, holding, use or disclosure of such information. The amendment included electronic data.

- Education and Skills Act (2008) aimed to increase participation in learning for young people and adults. It puts in place a right for adults to basic and inter-mediate skills, giving adults a second chance to gain the skills they need to thrive in society and throughout their working lives.

- Equality Act (2010) brings disability, sex, race and other grounds of discrimi-nation within one piece of legislation. See Chapter 3 for further information.

- Freedom of Information Act (2000) gives students the opportunity to request to see the information your organisation holds about them.

- Health and Safety at Work etc Act (1974) (HASAWA) imposes obligations on all staff within an organisation commensurate with their role and responsibil-ity. Risk assessments should be carried out where necessary. In the event of an accident, particularly one resulting in death or serious injury, an investiga-tion by the Health and Safety Executive may result in the prosecution of indi-viduals found to be negligent as well as the organisation.

- Human Rights Act (1998) gives all people basic rights. All public bodies are required to adhere to the Act and the courts must interpret UK law in accor-dance with the European Convention on Human Rights and Fundamental Freedoms.

- Protection of Children Act (POCA) (1999) was designed to protect children. It gives responsibility to local authorities to make enquiries when anyone con-tacts them with concerns about child abuse. You will need to be checked by the Criminal Records Bureau (CRB) if you are teaching children or vulnerable adults.

- Safeguarding Vulnerable Groups Act (2006) introduced a vetting and barring scheme to make decisions about who should be barred from working with children and vulnerable adults. You will need to have a CRB check before you can teach children or vulnerable adults.

- The Further Education Teachers' Qualifications (England) Regulations (2007) brought in revised teaching qualifications for new teachers and a professional status for all teachers in the further education sector in England. Teachers must register with the IfL and partake in CPD. Teachers should be qualified and hold QTLS or ATLS status within five years of taking a teaching position. See 'Progression' in Chapter 7 for further details.

Specific

These will differ depending upon the subject and environment within which you teach. Examples of specific legislation and codes of practice are as follows.

- Control of Substances Hazardous to Health (COSHH) Regulations (2002) if you work with hazardous materials.

- Food Hygiene Regulations (2006) apply to aspects of farming, manufacturing, distributing and retailing food.

- Health and Safety (Display Screen Equipment) Regulations (1992) if you use display screen equipment.

- Information Technology Codes of Practice relate to the use of computers in your particular organisation: for example, internet access and e-mail protocol.

- Management of Health and Safety at Work Regulations (1999) aim to prevent unsafe practices and minimise risks.

- Manual Handling Operations Regulations (1992) relate to hazards of manual handling and risks of injury.

- Reporting of Injuries, Diseases and Dangerous Occurrences (RIDDOR) Regulations (1995) – specified workplace incidents must be reported.

Following the required legislation and codes of practice, and carrying out your roles and responsibilities to the best of your ability, will help ensure you become an effective and professional teacher.

Extension Activity

Identify and research the legislation and codes of practice relevant to your subject area and the context/environment within which you will teach. Summarise the key aspects of these and state how they could impact upon your role.

Summary

In this chapter you have learnt about:

- roles and responsibilities of a teacher
- boundaries of teaching
- record keeping
- legislation and codes of practice.

Cross-referencing grid

This chapter contributes towards the following: scope (S), knowledge (K) and practice (P) aspects of the Professional Teaching Standards (A–F domains) and the PTLLS units' assessment criteria. Full details of the learning outcomes and assessment criteria for each PTLLS unit can be found in the appendices.

Domain	Standards
A	ASI, AS6, AS7, AK2.1, AK2.2, AK4.2, AK6.1, AK6.2, AK7.1, AK7.2, AP6.1, AP6.2, AP7.1
B	BS2, BK1.3, BK2.7, BP2.7
C	CSI, CS3, CS4, CKI.1, CKI.2, CK4.1, CPI.1
D	
E	
F	FS2, FK2.1, FP2.1

PTLLS unit	Assessment criteria	
	Level 3	Level 4
Roles, responsibilities and relationships in lifelong learning	1.1, 1.3, 1.4 2.1, 2.3 3.1	1.1, 1.3, 1.4 2.1, 2.3 3.1
Understanding inclusive learning and teaching in lifelong learning		
Using inclusive learning and teaching approaches in lifelong learning		
Principles of assessment in lifelong learning	3.1	3.1

Theory focus

References and further information

Francis, M and Gould, J (2009) *Achieving Your PTLLS Award*. London: Sage Publications Ltd.

HMI (2004) *Every Child Matters: Change for Children*. London: DfES.

IfL (2008) *Code of Professional Practice*. London: Institute for Learning.

LLUK (2006) *New Overarching Professional Standards for Teachers, Tutors and Trainers in the Lifelong Learning Sector*. London: Skills for Business.

Reece, I and Walker, S (2008) *Teaching Training and Learning: A Practical Guide* (6th edn). Tyne & Wear: Business Education Publishers Ltd.

Tummons, J (2010) *Becoming a Professional Tutor in the Lifelong Learning Sector* (2nd edn). Exeter: Learning Matters.

Wilson, L (2008) *Practical Teaching: A Guide to PTLLS and CTLLS*. London: Cengage Learning.

Websites

All government legislation and regulations – www.opsi.gov.uk
Criminal Records Bureau – www.crb.gov.uk
Institute for Learning – www.ifl.ac.uk
Office for Standards in Education – www.ofsted.gov.uk

Introduction

In this chapter you will learn about:

- the teaching and learning environment
- learning styles
- key theories of learning
- motivation

There are activities and examples to help you reflect on the above which will assist your understanding of some of the key theories of learning. At the end of each section is an extension activity to stretch and challenge your learning further.

At the end of the chapter is a cross-referencing grid showing how the chapter's contents contribute towards the professional teaching standards and PTLLS units.

The teaching and learning environment

A suitable learning environment is crucial for effective learning to take place. This involves not only the venue and resources used, but also your attitude and the support you give to your students. Learning can take place in a variety of contexts: for example, further education and sixth-form colleges, the workplace, adult and community learning centres, training organisations, the forces, public, private and voluntary sectors, prisons, industry and commerce. While learning can take place almost anywhere, not all environments will be totally suitable; however, it's how you teach your subject that will make learning effective. If you can convey passion and enthusiasm you will help motivate your students to want more.

You may be restricted by the availability of some rooms or resources; therefore you need to be imaginative with what you do have. Your students don't need to know any problems your organisation has, as your professionalism should enable you to teach your subject effectively. However, you do need to take into account any health and safety issues and let your organisation know of any concerns. You need to establish a purposeful learning environment where your students feel safe, secure, confident and valued. The venue, toilets and refreshment areas should be accessible to and suitable for everyone. If your session includes a break, make sure you tell your students what time this will be and for how long. If you don't, students may not be concentrating on their learning but thinking about when they can go to the toilet or get a drink.

If you are teaching a practical subject, you will need a suitable environment so that you can demonstrate and your students can practise, for example, a workshop or laboratory. If you are teaching a theoretical subject, you may be fine in a classroom but you might need a computer, projector and interactive whiteboard. You might be delivering a seminar in a venue you have never visited before. If this is the case, it would be useful to telephone or visit in advance to check what facilities are available. Creating a good first impression, being organised and professional should help your students feel they are in good hands.

Room layouts

The environment has three aspects: physical, social and learning. Each has an impact on the others and is equally important when planning your sessions. The physical environment is about the surroundings within which learning takes place; this need not be a traditional classroom but could be outdoors or another setting such as a community centre. The temperature, lighting and the area designated for learning can all affect the learning that takes place. You may need to close blinds to block out the sun, open a window to let in fresh air or even tidy rubbish away that has been left by the previous occupiers. The social environment is about how you put your students at ease, establish a rapport with them and help them work together. The learning environment is concerned with giving your session a sense of purpose and direction by having clear aims, using suitable teaching and learning approaches, resources and assessment methods.

If you are teaching indoors, an important influence upon the way your session progresses and how you and your students can communicate will be the room layout. You may not be able to control this if the furniture is in fixed positions. However, if you can, it is best to create an environment where students can communicate with each other and see everything you are doing. You should move around the room regularly and interact with your students rather than stay at the front or behind a desk.

Desks in rows

This traditional classroom style does not lead to effective communication between students. However, all students can see the teacher as well as all presentation materials and resources being used. This layout is useful when delivering theoretical subjects if group work is not required. Students tend to sit in the same seats at each session; the first ones in often head for the tables at the back. This layout without the tables would enable more chairs to be positioned in rows, allowing many students to attend a session at the same time. This is known as lecture style. The teacher would need good voice projection to reach all students at the back of the room, or use a microphone. The chairs might have a moveable arm on which to rest notes. If a student is sitting in the middle of a row and needed to leave for any reason, they would disrupt the rest of the row of students. See Figure 2.1 below.

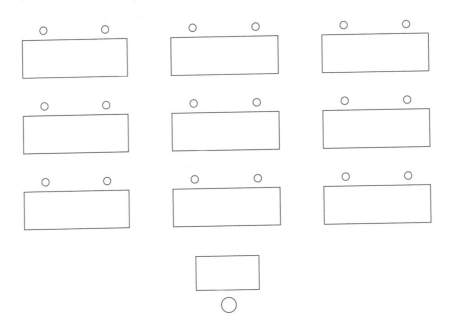

Figure 2.1 Desks in rows – classroom-style layout

Desks in groups

This *cabaret* style is much better to allow students to work together and interact during group activities. All students can still see the teacher and any presentation materials being used. If room permits, tables could be moved so that they are not so close together, or placed at different angles. The teacher could sit beside the desk rather than behind so as not to create a barrier, or move around the room while teaching. See Figure 2.2 opposite.

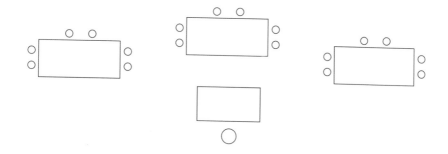

Figure 2.2 Cabaret-style layout

Horseshoe or U shape

This style allows for large group discussions between the students and the teacher, but is not good for small group work. Students can still see the teacher and any presentation materials being used. Students sitting at the very ends of tables may feel excluded from the group if activities are taking place. More tables could be added if necessary to close the gap and create an oblong shape; the teacher then becomes part of the group. See Figure 2.3 below.

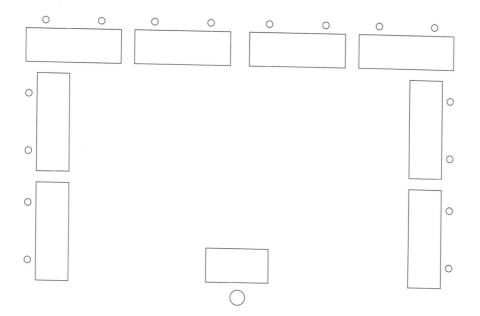

Figure 2.3 Horseshoe or U-shape layout

Boardroom style

This style allows for discussions and group work where a large table area is needed. If the teacher sits at the table with the students, everyone can communicate and see each other. If the teacher sits separately, some students will have their back to them and not be able to see a presentation screen if used. See Figure 2.4 below.

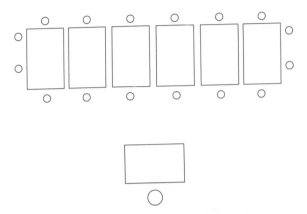

Figure 2.4 Boardroom-style layout

Other layouts

By experimenting with other layouts you can see how effective they are; for example, for individual, small group work and seminars. This can include the teacher as part of the group, with or without tables. Sometimes tables can create barriers between the teacher and the students. If you need to move furniture, you should get another member of staff to help you beforehand and again afterwards. You will need to allow space for movement around the room and for bags and coats, to ensure there are no obstructions. Always return the room to its original layout at the end of your session. See Figure 2.5 below.

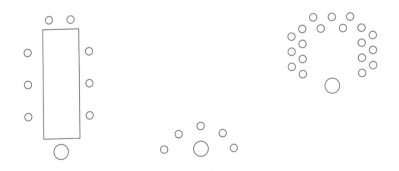

Figure 2.5 Other layouts

Activity

Think back to a really good, or a really bad experience you have had as a student. Explain how the physical and social aspects had an impact upon your learning. Were there any other aspects that influenced your learning? What can you do to ensure your students have a good experience with you?

You need to manage the learning environment to promote and encourage individual and group learning. The seating arrangements can have a big impact on learning. People like their comfort zones and you may find that students will sit in the same place each time they are with you. This is often the place they sat at during the first session. This is useful to help you remember their names as you can sketch a seating plan and make a note of them. Remembering and using students' names will show respect, and encourage them to talk to you in confidence if they have any concerns. Moving students around can either help or hinder their learning depending upon the group dynamics and student maturity.

If possible, arrive early to set up the environment as you may find it hasn't been left in a suitable condition by the previous user.

Example

Harry arrived at 10.25 a.m. ready for his session which commenced at 10.30 a.m. He found the room was untidy with rubbish on the floor, three chairs were missing, writing was on the board and the computer wasn't connected to the projector. He became very flustered, his students arrived while he was trying to prepare the room and he therefore didn't give a professional impression.

You need to ensure the physical environment is suitable not only for learning, but for social interaction too. If possible, aim for 70 per cent of the time for student involvement and 30 per cent of the time for your formal input. This will of course depend upon the subject you are teaching. However, setting activities, projects and group work for your students to carry out should aid the learning process and keep them interested and motivated. A research project known as the *Beginning Teacher Evaluation Study (BTES)* focused upon academic learning time (ALT) as a measure of learning. There have been many other studies which you might like to research further by using the references at the end of the chapter, or searching the internet for *academic learning time*.

Health and safety considerations

Learners are entitled to learn in a safe and healthy environment. Under the Health and Safety at Work etc Act 1974 (HASAWA), health and safety is your responsibility as well as your organisation's. If you see a potential hazard, do something about it; don't wait for an accident to happen. Your students may need to wear protective clothing or use hazardous substances for some activities; you will therefore need to find out what your organisation's procedures are for these. You might be using electrical equipment which will need regular checks by an appointed person in your organisation. You also need to make sure that any floor surfaces are not slippery, that any trailing wires are out of the way and any equipment your students will be working with is safe and reliable. If you are teaching a subject that could be dangerous or hazardous, you may need to carry out risk assessments which should be documented. You could include your students in this process to help them identify any issues or concerns, prior to their use.

You will need to know your organisation's accident and fire procedures such as the location of fire exits and meeting points, extinguishers and first aid facilities. You should inform your students of these during their first session with you. If you have any students who started late, you should always give them this information when they commence. You could include it in an induction handout or it may already be in a student handbook they have been given. The Learning and Skills Council (now called the Skills Funding Agency) produced guidance for students in the form of a handbook called *The Safe Learner (2007)*, which is a useful document to refer to when inducting your students.

You should familiarise yourself with your organisation's health and safety policy and any other relevant legislation. You may have students who have individual needs such as epilepsy or diabetes. It is important to know who they are, what you need to do, and who you need to contact in case of an emergency.

Extension Activity

Think about the subject you would like to teach and the environment you will teach in. Can you change anything to make the area more conducive to learning? What health and safety considerations might there be? Are there any restrictions regarding the resources your students need to use; for example, cutting equipment? How can you involve your students identifying any health and safety issues? Are there any records you need to complete beforehand or anyone you need to liaise with?

Learning styles

There is an old Chinese proverb: *I hear – I forget, I see – I remember, I do – I understand.* When you hear lots of information you may find it difficult to remember it all. If you can see something taking place that represents what you hear, you will hopefully remember more. However, if you actually carry out the task, you will understand the full process and remember how to do it again.

> *Studies show that over a period of three days, learning retention is as follows.*
> - *10% of what you read.*
> - *20% of what you hear.*
> - *30% of what you see.*
> - *50% of what you see and hear.*
> - *70% of what you say.*
> - *90% of what you say and you do.*
> (Pike, 1989)

If your students can incorporate reading, hearing, seeing, saying and doing during your sessions, their learning retention should increase.

Activity

Think about the subject you will teach. How can you ensure your students use reading, hearing, seeing, saying and doing something?

Once students put theory into practice they will begin to understand what they have learnt. Students also have a particular learning style, a way that helps them to learn which is based on seeing, listening, reading and doing. Your students could take a short learning styles test prior to commencing your programme to identify what their individual preferences are. However, what you may tend to do is teach your sessions in the style in which you learn best – although it will suit you, it may not suit your students. Sue Crowley of the IfL (LSIS, 2009, page 8) stated:

> *Often new teachers teach as they were taught, then perhaps as they would like to have been taught, and finally they realise different people learn in different ways and a wider spectrum of teaching and learning approaches are needed and available.*

Fleming (2005)

Fleming stated that people can be grouped into four styles of learning: visual, aural, read/write and kinaesthetic (VARK).

Visual
Visual (seeing) learners usually:

- are meticulous and neat in appearance
- find verbal instructions difficult
- memorise by looking at pictures
- notice details
- observe rather than act or talk
- like watching videos/DVDs.

Aural
Aural (listening and talking) learners usually:

- are easily distracted
- enjoy talking and listening to others
- have difficulty with written instructions

- hum, sing and whisper or talk out loud

- ask questions

- don't like noisy environments.

Read/write

Read/write (reading and writing) learners usually:

- are good spellers and have good handwriting

- enjoy research

- like rewriting what others have written

- like to read books

- use a dictionary and thesaurus

- write lists and make notes.

Kinaesthetic

Kinaesthetic (doing) learners usually:

- are tactile towards others

- do not like reading and are often poor spellers

- enjoy worksheets and discussions

- fidget with pens while studying

- like practical activities

- use their hands while talking.

Not all learners fall into one style they may be multi-modal, i.e. a mixture of two or more styles enabling learning to take place more quickly.

Honey and Mumford (1992)

Honey and Mumford suggest learners are a mixture of the four styles:

- activist

- pragmatist

- theorist

- reflector.

Activist

Activist learners like to deal with new problems and experiences and like lots of activities to keep them busy. They love challenges and are enthusiastic.

Pragmatist

Pragmatist learners like to apply what they have learnt to practical situations. They like logical reasons for doing something.

Theorist

Theorist learners need time to take in information, they prefer to read lots of material first. They like things that have been tried and tested.

Reflector

Reflector learners think deeply about what they are learning and the activities they could do to apply this learning. They will then try something and think again about it.

Activity

Consider something you have recently learnt: for example, using a new mobile phone. Did you: jump right in and press all the buttons (activist); look briefly at the instructions and then have a go (pragmatist); read the instructions thoroughly, then carry them out (theorist); or become confident at using the phone for calls and texts before considering its other uses (reflector)?

It is always useful to get your students to carry out a learning styles test. It can be fun and lead to an interesting discussion, as well as helping you plan your teaching and learning approaches to reach their learning styles. It also empowers students to adapt information in a way that they are comfortable with, for example, using a voice recorder rather than hand writing notes. However, there are critics of learning styles. Coffield states … *it was not sufficient to pay attention to individual differences in learners, we must take account of the whole teaching – learning environment.* (2008, 1 page 31)

Extension Activity

If you have access to the internet, log on to the website www.vark-learn.com and carry out the learning styles test. It only takes a few minutes and you will receive an instant result. Locate another suitable learning styles questionnaire and carry it out. Compare and contrast your results. Decide which test could be used with your own students and how you could make use of the results to help their learning. If you don't have internet access, research different learning styles in relevant textbooks.

Key theories of learning

Students need to know why it is important for them to learn, what they are going to learn and how they will do this. Setting clear aims of what you want your students to achieve is the starting point; summarising regularly, varying your teaching approaches and taking learning styles into account will all help. Having a sense of humour and making learning interesting and fun will help your students remember key points. Your students need to believe that what they are learning has real value and meaning. You also need to treat each student as an individual and with respect, using their name wherever possible. You should always introduce yourself to your students; you could keep your name visible somewhere or wear a name badge. This should encourage them to approach you or ask questions.

There are lots of theories regarding how people learn. These theories will have been based on ideas, thoughts and experiences. Some are quite old, but are tried and trusted; others are fairly recent. You may even come up with your own theory or challenge existing ones. All people learn differently, perhaps influenced by experiences in their childhood, school, personal or professional relationships. When you learn something new, you will probably adapt, change or modify your behaviour as a result, and the same will apply to your students. This section will briefly explain some of these theories, which you may wish to research further.

Sensory theory

Laird (1985) stated that learning occurs when the five senses of sight, hearing, touch, smell and taste are stimulated. Laird's theory suggests that if multi-senses are stimulated, greater learning takes place. You could therefore adapt your teaching styles and resources to enable your students to use as many of their senses as possible.

Example

When you were a child, if you saw something that interested you, you would touch it, probably putting it in your mouth if it was small, shaking it to hear if it made a noise and putting it near your nose to smell it. You would soon learn if something tasted nasty not to put it in your mouth again. Therefore, a change in your behaviour took place as a result.

Conditions of learning

Gagne (1985) stated that there are several different types or levels of learning. Each different type requires different types of teaching. Gagne identified five major conditions of learning. These are:

- verbal information
- intellectual skills
- cognitive strategies

- motor skills

- attitudes.

Different internal and external conditions are required for each category of learning. For example, for motor skills to be learnt, there must be the opportunity for your student to practise new skills rather than just learn about them. For attitudes, your student must be able to explore these: for example, discussing environmental issues. In addition, this theory outlines nine events that activate the processes needed for effective learning to take place. Gagne believed all teaching and learning sessions should include this sequence of events. Each has a corresponding cognitive process (in brackets below).

1. Gaining attention (reception).

2. Informing students of the objective (expectancy).

3. Stimulating recall of prior learning (retrieval).

4. Presenting the stimulus (selective perception).

5. Providing learning guidance (semantic encoding).

6. Eliciting performance (responding).

7. Providing feedback (reinforcement).

8. Assessing performance (retrieval).

9. Enhancing retention and transfer (generalisation).

Example

Sue can ensure all these events take place in her sessions by:

1. *Gaining attention – showing an example of what the students will achieve during the session, e.g. an iced wedding cake.*
2. *Identifying the objective – stating that the students will be able to ice a wedding cake by the end of the session.*
3. *Recalling prior learning – asking the students if they have ever iced a wedding cake before.*
4. *Presenting stimulus – explaining how they will ice the wedding cake and what they will need to use.*
5. *Guiding learning – demonstrating how to ice a wedding cake.*
6. *Eliciting performance – encouraging the students to begin icing a wedding cake.*
7. *Providing feedback – informing the students how they are progressing.*
8. *Assessing performance – ensuring the students are correctly icing the wedding cake by observing and asking questions.*
9. *Enhancing retention/transfer – summarising the learning relating it to real life events and explaining what will be covered in the next session.*

Experiential theory

Kolb (1984) proposed a four-stage experiential learning cycle by which people understand their experiences, and as a result, modify their behaviour. It is based on the idea that the more often a student reflects on a task, the more often they have the opportunity to modify and refine their efforts. See Figure 2.6 below.

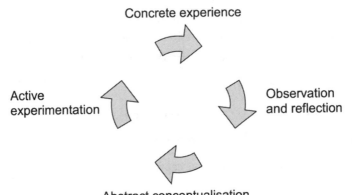

Figure 2.6 Kolb's (1984) experiential learning cycle

- Concrete experience is about experiencing or immersing yourself in the task and is the first stage in which a person simply carries out the task assigned. This is the *doing* stage.

- Observation and reflection involve stepping back from the task and reviewing what has been done and experienced. Your values, attitudes and beliefs can influence your thinking at this stage. This is the stage of *thinking* about what you have done.

- Abstract conceptualisation involves interpreting the events that have been carried out and making sense of them. This is the stage of *planning* how you will do it differently.

- Active experimentation enables you to take the new learning and predict what is likely to happen next or what actions should be taken to refine the way the task is done again. This is the *redoing* stage based upon experience and reflection.

The process of learning can begin at any stage and is continuous, i.e. there is no limit to the number of cycles you can make in a learning situation. This theory suggests that without reflection, people would continue to repeat their mistakes.

Example

Wang is taking an accounting programme which has an examination at the end. If he fails he will not know why he has failed. He will need to wait another three months before he can retake the examination. During the programme, he could experience the learning process, but not reflect upon what he might be doing wrong that may lead to him failing the examination. He therefore could not modify his behaviour and try again. If he took a programme with ongoing assessment instead of an examination at the end, he would have the opportunity to go through the full cycle. He would have the experience, reflect upon it due to ongoing feedback, think how he could improve and then experiment to try again.

You are probably familiar with the saying *you learn by experience*. You might find that doing a task, then thinking about it, leads you to plan how you would do it differently next time. Repeating tasks will help your students learn, whether this is a practical task or a theoretical subject.

Humanist theory

Rogers (1983) and others developed the theory of facilitative learning. This is based upon a belief that people have a natural eagerness to learn and that learning involves changing your own concept of yourself. This theory suggests that learning will take place if the person delivering it acts as a facilitator. They should establish an atmosphere in which their students feel comfortable and able to discuss new ideas, if they are not threatened by external factors.

Example

Vicky is due to teach a Digital Photography for Beginners evening class. There is no syllabus, therefore she has planned what she thinks is relevant, based on the last time she taught it. However, she remembered being told by an observer in her class last term that she should consider the needs of her students more. Therefore, at the first session, she has decided to encourage her students to tell her if they have anything they would like to learn, which she hadn't planned to teach. This will enable her to facilitate her sessions to cover their expectations and help make her students feel comfortable to discuss the topics.

Behaviourist theory

Skinner (1974) believed that behaviour is a function of its consequences. Your student will repeat the desired behaviour if positive reinforcement follows. If negative feedback is given, the behaviour should not be repeated. Giving immediate feedback, whether positive or negative, should enable your student to behave in a certain way.

Positive reinforcement or rewards can include verbal feedback such as *That's great, you've produced that document without any errors* or *You're certainly getting on well with that task* through to more tangible rewards such as a certificate at the end of the programme or a promotion or pay rise.

Example

Jamie was sawing a piece of wood and hadn't paid attention to the health and safety regulations. The saw kept slipping and he cut his hand. His teacher gave him negative feedback and this, along with his cut, ensured he was more careful in future.

The Peter principle

Peter and Hull (1969) stated that people are promoted to their highest level of competence, after which further promotion raises them to a level just beyond this and they become incompetent. These levels are as follows.

- Unconscious incompetence – you don't know how to do something, but don't know that you don't know this. To reach the next level, you need to know what it is that you don't know.
- Conscious incompetence – you know what you want to do, and start to appreciate the gap in your competence. To reach the next level you need to know how to become competent.
- Conscious competence – you can do what you set out to do, but have to give it a lot of attention. Through repeated practice you can reach the next level.
- Unconscious competence – you can perform a skill easily without giving it a great deal of thought. Once you achieve unconscious competence, you are at a level which suits your ability at the time. However, if you are promoted or try something different, you may return to the first level and become unconsciously incompetent again.

This is useful to know, as your students may reach and stay at one of these levels.

Example

Renuka has just started a Using Spreadsheets programme, having previously only used a computer for e-mails. She doesn't yet know how to use a spreadsheet or the functions it can perform – she is at the unconscious incompetence level. After learning how to set up a spreadsheet, she now wishes to perform some calculations; she knows she wants to do this but doesn't know how. This is the conscious incompetence level. Renuka soon learns how to perform calculations and practises this at the conscious competence level. She isn't quite at the unconscious competence level yet, where she could do it without thinking.

Domains of learning

Bloom (1956) stated that learning often goes through the following stages which should lead to a change in behaviour. These stages are:

- attention
- perception
- understanding
- short-/long-term memory
- change in behaviour.

These stages can affect your students' thinking, emotions and actions, and Bloom called them domains: cognitive, affective and psycho-motor (respectively). Think of cognitive as the head (thinking), affective as the heart (emotions) and psycho-motor as the hands (actions).

When teaching your subject, you need to consider which domain you want to reach, for example:

- cognitive (subject – geography) students will state the reasons for coastal erosion
- affective (subject – the environment) students will discuss their ideas for recycling
- psycho-motor (subject – bricklaying) students will build a two-foot high wall.

You will also need to consider how you can address all learning styles, particularly if your subject is a practical one and the majority of your students are read/write.

Extension Activity

Compare and contrast two or more of the learning theories in this section. How will they affect the way you teach and the way your students will learn? Research other learning theories such as those which come under the headings of pragmatists and constructivists.

Motivation

You need to be aware of what motivates your students, as their keenness to learn will affect their learning and behaviour during your sessions. A student attending a session because they have been told to may not be as motivated as a student who is there for personal fulfilment.

Motivation is either intrinsic (from within), meaning the student wants to learn for their own fulfilment, or extrinsic (from without), meaning there may be an external factor motivating the student: for example, a promotion at work.

Whatever level of motivation your students have will be transformed, for better or worse, by what happens during their learning experience with you. You therefore need to promote a professional relationship that leads to individual learning and trust. Some students may seem naturally enthusiastic about learning, but many need or expect you to inspire, challenge, engage and stimulate them.

Many factors affect a student's motivation to work and to learn: for example, interest in the subject matter, perception of its usefulness, a general desire to achieve, self-confidence and self-esteem, as well as patience and persistence. Not all students are motivated by the same values, needs, desires, or wants. Some of your students will be motivated by the approval of others and some by overcoming personal challenges.

To help motivate your students you can:

- ask open questions, not closed questions, which just lead to yes or no responses
- avoid creating intense competition, although some competition can be challenging and fun
- be aware of their attention-span limits
- challenge and support those who need it
- give ongoing constructive feedback
- maintain an organised and orderly atmosphere
- make tasks interesting, practical and relevant
- negotiate clear targets
- treat them with respect and as individuals
- vary your teaching approaches to reach all learning styles
- give praise and encouragement.

Attention spans

An attention span is the amount of time that a student can concentrate without being distracted. This will vary due to the age of your students; younger students will concentrate less and older ones more. Being able to focus without being distracted is crucial for learning to take place. There are two types of attention, *focused* and *sustained*.

- Focused attention is a short-term response to something that attracts awareness and is very brief. For example, the ring of a telephone or an unexpected occurrence. After a few seconds, it is likely that the person will return to what they were originally doing or think about something else.

- Sustained attention is a longer-term response which will enable the achievement of something over a period of time. For example, if the task is to take a few photos, choose the best three and upload them to a website, then the person showing sustained attention will stay on task and achieve it. A person who loses attention might take a few photos but move on to doing something else before choosing and uploading the best three.

Most healthy teenagers and adults are able to sustain attention on one thing for about 20 minutes (Cornish and Dukette, 2009, page 73). They can then choose to refocus on the same thing for another 20 minutes. This ability to renew concentration enables people to stay on task for as long as necessary. However, there are other factors to take into consideration, such as self-motivation, ability, tiredness and hunger. If a student is really hungry their concentration may lapse as a result. If you find your students losing focus, ask them if there's anything distracting them as you might be able to resolve it, for example, opening a window if it's too warm.

When planning to deliver your sessions, try and use lots of short tasks to enable your students to stay focused. If you do need to use longer tasks, try and break these down into 20 minutes for each, with a chance of a discussion or something different in between. If you teach long sessions, for example over an hour, try and include a break to enable your students to experience a change of scenery, obtain refreshments and visit the toilet if necessary.

Activity

Plan a task to carry out with your students which will take 20 minutes. If possible, carry out the activity and observe how many students stay on task or get easily distracted. If they are distracted, ask them why this was and then use their responses to improve the task for the future.

You might find that attention spans are decreasing due to the use of modern technology. For example, searching the internet, changing television channels and using electronic devices and mobile phones can reduce concentration time. If you have students who have been brought up in the digital age, they may have reduced attention spans and need to move on to other tasks more frequently. If applicable, you could incorpoate ICT, for example researching current topics.

Maslow (1987) introduced a *Hierarchy of Needs* in 1954 after rejecting the idea that human behaviour was determined by childhood events. He felt that obstacles should be removed that prevent a person from achieving their goals. He argued there are five needs which represent different levels of motivation which must be met. The highest level was labelled *self-actualisation*, meaning people are fully functional, possess a healthy personality, and take responsibility for themselves and their actions. He also believed that people should be able to move through these needs to the highest level provided they are given an education that promotes growth.

Figure 2.7 below shows the needs expressed as they might relate to learning, starting at the base of the pyramid.

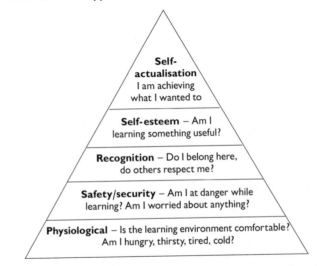

Self-actualisation
I am achieving what I wanted to

Self-esteem – Am I learning something useful?

Recognition – Do I belong here, do others respect me?

Safety/security – Am I at danger while learning? Am I worried about anything?

Physiological – Is the learning environment comfortable? Am I hungry, thirsty, tired, cold?

Figure 2.7 Maslow's (1987) Hierarchy of needs expressed in educational terms

When students satisfy their needs at one level, they should be able to progress to the next. Something may set them back a level, but they will keep striving upwards. It is these needs that motivate learning to take place. However, some people may not want to progress through the levels, and may be quite content where they are at that moment in their life.

To help your students' motivation, always ensure that the learning environment you create meets your students' first-level needs. This will enable them to feel comfortable and secure enough to learn and progress to the higher levels. You will need to appreciate that some students may not have these lower needs met in their home lives, making it difficult for them to move on to the higher levels.

Always try to establish a purposeful learning environment where your students can feel safe, secure, confident and valued.

Example

Ruth was due to teach a session from 5 p.m. to 7 p.m. She arrived early and noticed the room was hot and stuffy so opened the windows. She also realised that most of her students might not have had a chance to eat something prior to the session. When they arrived she told them they could have an early break to enable them to get refreshments. After break, she kept one window open to keep some fresh air in the room and also allowed her students to have bottled water if they wished. This ensured her students' first-level needs were met.

While you may be very good at teaching your subject, you might have no control over the environment and will need to create a suitable atmosphere. Your enthusiasm and passion for your subject will help engage your learners. If you can also make your session interesting and varied, your learners will enjoy the experience and remember more about the subject and you, rather than the environment or lack of facilities.

Extension Activity

Research other motivation theorists such as Elton Mayo (1880–1949) Hawthorne Effect theory, Frederick Herzberg (1923–2000) Two factor theory and Douglas McGregor (1906–1964) X and Y theory. Compare and contrast these. How will their theories affect the way you motivate your students? What are your own theories of motivation?

Summary

In this chapter you have learnt about:

- the teaching and learning environment
- learning styles
- key theories of learning
- motivation.

Cross-referencing grid

This chapter contributes towards the following: scope (S), knowledge (K) and practice (P) aspects of the Professional Teaching Standards (A–F domains) and the PTLLS units' assessment criteria. Full details of the learning outcomes and assessment criteria for each PTLLS unit can be found in the appendices.

Domain	Standards
A	ASI, AS2, AKI.I, AK2.I, AK2.2, AK4.I, API.I, AP2.2, AP3.I, AP4.I, AP6.2
B	BSI, BKI.I, BKI.2, BKI.3, BK2.I, BK2.2, BK2.3, BPI.I, BPI.3
C	CK3.I, CP3.I
D	
E	
F	

PTLLS unit	Assessment criteria	
	Level 3	Level 4
Roles, responsibilities and relationships in lifelong learning	3.I	3.I
Understanding inclusive learning and teaching in lifelong learning	3.I	3.I
Using inclusive learning and teaching approaches in lifelong learning		
Principles of assessment in lifelong learning		

Theory focus

References and further information

Bloom, BS (1956) *Taxonomy of Educational Objectives: The Classification of Educational Goals*. New York: McKay.

Carr, N (2010) The Web Shatters Focus, Rewires Brains. *Wired magazine*, 24 May. Available at: www.wired.com/magazine/2010/05/ff_nicholas_carr/all/I (accessed October 2011).

Coffield, F (2008) *Just Suppose Teaching and Learning Became the First Priority*. London: LSN.

Cornish, D and Dukette, D (2009) *The Essential 20: Twenty Components of an Excellent Health Care Team*. Pittsburgh: RoseDog Books.

Denham, C and Lieberman, A (1980) *A Time to learn: A Review of the Beginning Teacher Evaluation Study*. National Institute of Education.

Fisher, CW (1978) *The Beginning Teacher Evaluation Study*. California: National Institute of Education.

Fleming, N (2005) *Teaching and Learning Styles: VARK strategies*. Honolulu: Honolulu Community College.

Gagne, R (1985) *The Conditions of Learning* (4th edn). New York: Holt, Rinehart & Winston.

Honey, P and Mumford, A (1992) *The Manual of Learning Styles* (3rd edn). Maidenhead: Peter Honey Associates.

Kolb, DA (1984) *Experiential Learning: Experience as the Source of Learning and Development*. New Jersey: Prentice-Hall.

Laird, D (1985) *Approaches to Training and Development*. Harlow: Addison Wesley.

Learning and Skills Council (2007) *Student Health, Safety and Welfare: The Safe Learner Blueprint*. Coventry: LSC.

LSIS (2009) *Centres for Excellence in Teacher Training: CETT Standard*. Learning and Skills Improvement Service Newsletter issue 1.

Maslow, AH (1987) (edited by Frager, R) *Motivation and Personality* (3rd revised edn). New York: Pearson Education Ltd.

Peter, LJ and Hull, R (1969) *The Peter Principle: Why Things Always Go Wrong*. New York: William Morrow and Company.

Pike, RW (1989) *Creative Training Techniques Handbook*. Minneapolis MN: Lakewood Books.

Rogers, CR (1983) *Freedom to Learn for the 80s*. Columbus, OH: Merrill.

Skinner, BF (1974) *About Behaviorism*. San Francisco, CA: Knopf.

Wallace, S (2007) *Managing Behaviour in the Lifelong Learning Sector* (2nd edn). Exeter: Learning Matters.

Websites

Attention Spans – http://news.bbc.co.uk/1/hi/1834682.stm

Cognitive learning styles – http://tip.psychology.org/styles.html

Health and Safety Executive – www.hse.gov.uk

Informal Education Encyclopaedia – www.infed.org/encyclopaedia.htm

Learning styles test – www.vark-learn.com

Learning theories – www.learning-theories.com

Pragmatists and constructivists – http://classweb.gmu.edu/ndabbagh/Resources/IDKB/models_theories.htm

Time & Learning theory – www.timeandlearning.org/?q=node/16

Introduction

> In this chapter you will learn about:
>
> - identifying needs of the organisation, teachers and students
> - initial and diagnostic assessment
> - potential needs of students and points of referral
> - equality and diversity
> - inclusive learning

There are activities and examples to help you reflect on the above which will assist your understanding of how to identify the needs of the organisation, teachers and students. At the end of each section there are extension activities to stretch and challenge your learning further.

At the end of the chapter is a cross-referencing grid showing how the chapter's contents contribute towards the professional teaching standards and PTLLS units.

Identifying needs of the organisation, teachers and students

Identifying and understanding the needs of all parties involved in the teaching and learning process will help ensure your practice is effective.

Organisational needs

The starting point for planning teaching and learning is usually based upon the needs of your organisation: for example, the curriculum which is to be offered. The qualifications and programmes which make up the curriculum might be decided by local needs: for example, business and employment. Other considerations may include funding from external agencies, as some programmes are offered only if financial support can be obtained. External agencies such as awarding organisations will give approval for accredited qualifications to be delivered at your organisation. They will produce a syllabus or qualification handbook for each subject which gives details of what must be taught and assessed. If students successfully achieve the requirements, they will receive a certificate endorsed by the awarding organisation. Your organisation will recruit relevant experienced staff to meet their curriculum needs.

If there is a demand, *bespoke* programmes could be created to meet a particular need and be offered in house: for example, at a place of employment. These are known as *non-accredited* programmes and your organisation may issue certificates of attendance. These will prove a person was there, but not that they necessarily learnt anything. Assessment would need to take place to determine what that person actually learnt, enabling a certificate of competence to be issued. These types of programme are often classed as *full cost* and are paid for by the employer or the student.

Programmes and qualifications can be short-, medium- or long-term and may be offered at various times of the day or evening, at various locations, depending upon needs. Different models of delivery can be used such as formal attendance, open, on-line, distance learning, flexible, or blended learning which combines technology with learning.

If the programme you teach is advertised on your organisation's website, in a prospectus, leaflets or in the local press, make sure you read it to check it is correct. If what you plan to teach is different from that advertised, there will be confusion when your students commence.

Different models of delivery will influence what you must and could teach to your students. The *product* model focuses upon the outcomes of a programme: for example, what students need to know to pass an examination, test or assignment. The teacher often just teaches what must be taught to get the student through. What could be taught isn't taken into consideration, often due to time constraints, and doesn't benefit the learner in the long term.

Example

Samantha is taking GCSE French and just wants to pass the qualification. Her teacher covers only what is in the syllabus (what must be taught) and does not cover anything else which could help Samantha if she visits France in the future (what could be taught).

The *process* model focuses on the content of the programme and other relevant knowledge and skills that could be learnt and applied.

Example

Kelly is taking a word-processing qualification. She is paying for the programme herself and is prepared to continue until she feels competent. As she has never used a computer before, she has asked her teacher to help her learn keyboard skills and file-management skills. These are in addition to word-processing skills. She is therefore getting the benefit of what could be taught as well as what must be taught.

When planning what to teach, you will need to use the syllabus as your starting point, ensuring you teach all the required content. Additional aspects that could be taught to add value to the content will be based upon how much time you have and the needs of your organisation and students.

Teacher needs

All teachers should be not only knowledgeable and current in their subject knowledge but they should also know how to use innovative ways to teach their subject and enable learning to take place. Your needs as a teacher might include updating your subject knowledge, working towards teaching qualifications and/or learning new skills. This will all count towards your CPD which is a requirement of the IfL.

> *CPD gives the public, learners, the teaching community and the sector confidence that teachers, trainers, tutors and assessors are continuously improving their skills, knowledge and expertise. CPD is the hallmark of the professional.*
> (Institute for Learning, 2009)

You need a suitable environment in which to teach your subject. You may not be able to change the setting; however, you could make it more stimulating by displaying posters or changing the layout of the furniture (if possible). You will also need various resources to teach your subject effectively: for example, computers, models, books, etc. Whether you can have these might depend upon the finances available. If your organisation can't afford to buy up-to-date textbooks you could place the onus upon your students to purchase them or access them from the local library.

There are certain things you must know: for example, what and who you will be teaching, for how long, where and when. Knowing this will help you plan your sessions effectively. You will also need to know the people at your organisation who can support you: for example, administration staff and caretakers. When you start teaching, you should have a mentor, someone in the same subject area as yourself. They should show you around the premises, introduce you to relevant staff members and give you advice and support as necessary. If you encounter situations with students that you can't deal with, you must approach someone who can help you.

You might find it useful to create a toolkit of items you will regularly use when teaching. This could contain pens, board markers, a wireless remote control for electronic presentations, paper, a small clock, stapler, hole punch and other relevant items. It's useful to have a few extra pre-prepared activities or quizzes that you could use if you have spare time at the end of sessions, or if some students finish an activity earlier than others.

Student needs

Identifying your students' needs can take place as part of the application process, during an interview or when they commence the programme. Information, advice and guidance (IAG) should be given to students regarding their programme choice and this should be clear, unambiguous and impartial to ensure it meets their needs and capability. Identifying any individual student needs prior to commencement will help you plan your teaching to meet these. However, depending upon the type of programme you are teaching, you might not always be able to do this in advance. As a result, some students may take a programme which is unsuitable for them. If possible, try to have contact with all students before they are committed to taking a particular qualification.

Activity

Find out what the IAG procedures are at your organisation. How will you be involved with this process and how will it benefit your students? If you are not yet teaching, how do you think IAG staff can support students effectively?

Some students may be embarrassed or not wish to divulge personal information on application forms or at an interview. You could have an informal chat with them to find out if they have any needs or specific requirements: for example, dyslexia or dyscalculia. If you are unsure about how to help your students, just ask, as they are best placed to know how you could support them.

If you have a student requiring support for any reason, there is a difference between *learning support* and *student support*. Learning support relates to the subject, or help with literacy, language, numeracy or ICT skills. Student support relates to help they might need with any personal issues, and/or general advice and guidance.

You should discuss the requirements of the qualification with your students, along with the range of services and agencies that are available to assist with any specific needs. Impartial advice should also be available regarding career progression, job search, preparation for interviews and more. Your students will benefit greatly from this service and will be more likely to finish the programme and successfully achieve their qualification.

Extension Activity

Imagine you are a new teacher in a large college and have just achieved your PTLLS Award but have not taught your subject before. Three weeks before you are due to start teaching, you have an hour's meeting with your mentor. Your mentor is qualified in the same subject as you and has been teaching for five years at the same organisation. What questions would you want to ask them and why?

Initial and diagnostic assessment

This is the formal way of ascertaining your students' prior skills and/or knowledge of the subject to be taken and whether they have any specific needs. It should be carried out prior to, or at the beginning of, the programme. There could be particular entry requirements for your subject and an initial assessment or interview would ascertain if these had been met. Diagnostic assessments can be used to evaluate a student's skills, knowledge, strengths and areas for development in a particular area. It could be that your student feels they are capable of achieving at a higher level than the initial assessments determine. The results will give a thorough indication of not only the level at which your student needs to be placed for their subject but also which specific aspects they need to improve on. Diagnostic tests can also be used to ascertain information regarding literacy, language, numeracy and computer skills. Information gained from these tests will help you plan your sessions to meet any individual needs and/or to arrange further training and support if necessary. You should not take students just because you need the numbers to make a group. The programme may not be suitable for them and they may leave, therefore wasting their time and yours.

Using initial assessments will help you to identify any particular aspects which may otherwise go unnoticed and ensure you are meeting equality and diversity requirements.

Identifying learning styles as part of initial assessment will help you decide the teaching and learning approaches to use (see Chapter 2).

Initial assessment will:

- allow for differentiation and individual requirements to be met
- ensure students are on the right programme at the right level
- ensure the student knows what is expected of them
- identify an appropriate pace at which each student will progress

- identify an appropriate starting point for each student
- identify any information which needs to be shared with colleagues
- identify any specific additional support needs
- identify learning styles
- identify previous experience, achievements and transferable skills
- identify specific requirements: for example, literacy, numeracy and computer skills
- inspire and motivate students
- involve students, giving them confidence to negotiate suitable targets.

The results of initial assessments should help you negotiate individual learning plans (ILPs) or action plans with your students, ensuring they are on the right programme at the right level.

Extension Activity

Find out what initial and diagnostic assessments are used at your organisation. Will it be your responsibility to administer these, or is there a specialist person to do this? How will you use the results? If you are not yet teaching, research suitable ones that you could use with your students in future.

Potential needs of students and points of referral

Some students will have needs, barriers or challenges to learning that may affect their attendance and/or achievement. Hopefully you can ascertain these prior to your students commencing. However, others may occur during the programme and you would need to plan a suitable course of action to help the students, or refer them to an appropriate specialist or agency. You could keep a record of students whom you are concerned about, i.e. a *risk register*. You can update it with any issues or occurrences to keep track of progress before anything serious occurs.

Behaviour Code 3 of the IfL Code of Professional Practice states:

> *Members shall take reasonable care to ensure the safety and welfare of learners and comply with relevant statutory provisions to support their wellbeing and development.*

(IfL, 2008)

It's difficult to help your students if they don't tell you about any specific issues, needs or concerns they might have. You could ask if there is anything you could do to help make their learning experience a more positive one. However, anything you do would have to be reasonable, and not seen as favouritism by other students. Encouraging them to tell you when you are on your own at an appropriate time would save your student any embarrassment they might feel when in front of their peers.

If you can be proactive and notice potential needs before they become issues, you might be able to alleviate your students' concerns. Otherwise, you will need to be reactive to the issue and deal with it professionally and sensitively. Your students may trust you and tell you something confidential; however, you may need to pass this information on to more experienced people, particularly if your student is vulnerable and/or in need of expert help. See Table 3.1 below.

Table 3.1 Examples of potential needs, barriers and challenges

• abilities	• lack of confidence, motivation, social skills
• access to or fear of technology	• lack of resources
• age	• lack of support
• behavioural difficulties	• language
• bullying in person and cyber-bullying	• learning difficulties and disabilities
• childcare arrangements	• limited basic skills such as literacy, numeracy and ICT
• culture and language differences	• mental health issues
• disabilities	• mixed-ability learning styles
• discipline	• mobility problems
• dyslexia, dyscalculia, dyspraxia, etc.	• past experiences
• emotional or psychological problems	• peer pressure
• environment	• personal/work/home circumstances
• faith and religion	• physical, medical, mental or health conditions
• family commitments	• poor attendance
• fears: for example, technology, change, not knowing anyone else, previous school experiences	• previous learning experiences
• finance	• social problems
• hearing or visual impairment	• status of the group
• housing problems	• timing issues
• hyperactivity	• transport problems
	• weather

Points of referral

You may encounter students with varying degrees of needs; therefore you should remain impartial, but sensitive. You may feel you can deal with some of these yourself; however, it's best to seek advice or refer your student to someone who can help. You might experience students with a variety of issues, for example eating disorders, depression, attention deficit hyperactivity disorder (ADHD), dyslexia, physical or mental health problems, etc.

You should always refer your students to an appropriate specialist or agency if you can't deal with their needs. Never feel you have to solve any student problems yourself and don't get personally involved. You will need to find out what is available internally within your organisation or where you could refer them externally. See Table 3.2 opposite.

Example

Dave informed his teacher that he is dyslexic and asked if any handouts could be printed on cream paper. He also asked if anyone minded if he used a digital recorder during the sessions, as he preferred to listen to this afterwards rather than make notes. His teacher asked the group if they were all happy to have handouts on cream paper and whether they minded Dave recording the session. All the group agreed to his requests. The teacher also uploaded all the programme materials to the virtual learning environment (VLE). This enabled everyone to access and save or print them in a suitable format.

Table 3.2 Example points of referral

Internal	External
<ul><li>accommodation officers</li><li>careers advisers</li><li>colleagues</li><li>counsellors</li><li>examination officers</li><li>financial services staff</li><li>first-aiders</li><li>health and welfare officers</li><li>information, advice and guidance staff</li><li>interpreters</li><li>learning support staff</li><li>mentors</li><li>student support staff</li><li>student union representatives</li><li>teachers</li></ul>	<ul><li>awarding organisations</li><li>banks or building societies</li><li>carers</li><li>charities</li><li>childcare agencies</li><li>Citizens Advice Bureau</li><li>employers</li><li>health centres, slimming clubs, general practitioners, hospitals</li><li>Job Centre Plus</li><li>motoring and transport organisations</li><li>police</li><li>telephone helplines and agencies such as abuse, alcohol, bereavement support, Childline, Crimestoppers, debt, drug, lesbian and gay switchboard, gambling, NHS Direct, parentline, Samaritans, victim support</li><li>websites which are relevant</li></ul>

Extension Activity

What potential needs, barriers or challenges do you feel students might have? If you are currently teaching, find out what relevant points of referral are available to meet these needs, and review how effective they might be.

Equality and diversity

Equality is about the rights of students to have access to, attend, and participate in their chosen learning experience. This should be regardless of age, ability and/or circumstances. Any inequality and discrimination should be tackled to ensure fairness, decency and respect among your students. Equal opportunity is a concept underpinned by legislation to provide relevant and appropriate access for the participation, development and advancement of all individuals and groups. In the past, equality has often been described as *everyone being the* same or *having the same opportunities*. Nowadays, it can be described as *everyone being different, but having equal rights*.

Diversity is about valuing and respecting the differences in students, regardless of age, ability and/or circumstances, or any other individual characteristics they may have. If you have two or more students, you will experience diversity. You may have a mixed group of students with different levels of experience who are aiming to achieve the same qualification but at a different level. You could therefore set different activities and targets for the different assessment criteria of the qualification.

When teaching, you should always ensure you:

- are non-judgemental
- challenge any direct or indirect discrimination, stereotyping, prejudice, harassment, bullying and biased attitudes by yourself or other students
- challenge your own values, attitudes and beliefs so that you are not imposing these upon your students
- do not have favourite students or give some more attention than others
- do not indulge the minority at the expense of the majority
- ensure particular groups are not offended: for example, faiths or religions
- ensure particular students are not disadvantaged or overly advantaged
- treat all students with respect and dignity
- use activities and assessments which are pitched at the right level
- use questions which are worded so as not to cause embarrassment to students.

Example

Jo has a group of 20 students taking a programme in Photography. The students are aged between 16 and 70, with a variety of cultural backgrounds. They are mainly male and have various past experiences of the subject. Two of Jo's students use a wheelchair and one is dyslexic. Jo always makes sure her students can access all the physical and online resources, and uses handouts and photographs which represent all aspects of society. For their next assignment, Jo has asked them to take three photographs of different objects to compare and contrast. The assignment has been planned not to discriminate against anyone, and is therefore inclusive to all as the students can choose their own objects and locations.

When teaching, you should try and embrace, embed and advance all aspects of equality and diversity. You could use pictures in handouts and presentations which reflect different abilities, ages, cultures, genders and races.

You can also help your students by organising the learning environment to enable ease of access around any obstacles (including other students' bags and coats), and around internal and external doors. If you are ever in doubt as to how to help a student, just ask them.

Incorporating activities based around equality and diversity and the local community and society within which your students live and work could help your students be more understanding and tolerant of each other. You also need to prepare them for the world outside their own living and working environment in case they move elsewhere in the future.

The Equality Act 2010

The Equality Act (2010) replaced all previous anti-discrimination legislation and consolidated it into one Act (England, Scotland and Wales). It provides rights for people not to be directly discriminated against or harassed because they have an association with a disabled person or because they are wrongly perceived as disabled.

To ensure you comply with the Equality Act 2010, you need to be proactive in all aspects of equality and diversity, and make sure your teaching style and resources promote and include all students in respect of nine protected characteristics:

- age
- disability
- gender
- gender identity
- race
- religion and belief
- sexual orientation
- marriage and civil partnership
- maternity and pregnancy.

You could create activities to carry out with your students such as debates or quizzes to help raise awareness, perhaps during the induction process or group tutorials. Wherever possible, try to use naturally occurring opportunities for discussion.

Example

Mary was teaching a catering programme to a mixed group of students from various backgrounds and faiths. As Chinese New Year was approaching she decided to use it as a theme and create different menus around it. This opened up a discussion about the Chinese culture, which the group found interesting and meaningful. She decided she would research other cultures, faiths and religions to incorporate them during her sessions throughout the year.

Other opportunities could include discussing events in the news such as racist attacks, or an issue in a particular television programme such as disability or ageism. Try to encourage students not to make assumptions: for example, *foreigners always take the jobs of British people*, or *mothers always take time off work to look after their children*. If conversations like these occur, take the opportunity to challenge them.

There are seven different *types of discrimination*:

- associative discrimination: direct discrimination against someone because they are associated with another person with a protected characteristic
- direct discrimination: discrimination because of a protected characteristic
- indirect discrimination: when a rule or policy which applies to everyone can disadvantage a person with a protected characteristic
- discrimination by perception: direct discrimination against someone because others think they have a protected characteristic
- harassment: behaviour deemed offensive by the recipient
- harassment by a third party: the harassment of staff or others by people not directly employed by an organisation, such as an external consultant or visitor
- victimisation: discrimination against someone because they made or supported a complaint under equality legislation.

Extension Activity

How can you promote equality and value diversity within your sessions? Design an activity you could use with your students which encompasses some of the nine protected characteristics from the bulleted list above.

Inclusive learning

Inclusive learning is about involving all your students, treating them equally and fairly, without directly or indirectly excluding anyone. Some students could feel excluded during your session if their particular needs were not met. You therefore need to know in advance, through initial assessment or the induction process, just what these needs are. Inclusion is also about attitudes as well as behaviour, as students can be affected by the words or actions of others. You are not teaching your subject to a group of students who are all the same, but to a group of individuals with different experiences, abilities and needs which should be recognised and respected. Try to promote a positive culture of equality of opportunity within your sessions whereby all students can attend, participate and feel safe and valued. However, there may be occasions when you need to exclude a student from a session, for example, due to bullying.

Example

Tariq has a group of 16 students of different levels of experience and ability. He ensures each of his sessions includes a group activity where the full group is split into smaller groups of four students who will research and present a topic. Tariq ensures each group is made up of different students each time, which enables all students to get to know and work with each other, and share experiences. He gives each group member responsibility for an aspect of the activity, which ensures all members of the group must work together to achieve the task. This way, all his students are included in the activity and play an active part.

Using your students' names when talking to them, using eye contact and speaking personally to them during each session will help ensure they feel included. See Table 3.3 on page 58.

If you can develop the conditions for learning that are based on respect and trust and address the needs of individual students, you will have created an effective teaching and learning environment.

Extension Activity

Research inclusion in education via the internet or in textbooks and compare and contrast the definitions. Explain how you would promote inclusive learning with your students for your own specialist subject.

Table 3.3 Ways of promoting inclusion

Identifying needs	• ascertaining individual needs, learning styles and goals • ensuring all students can complete application and enrolment forms: for example, different languages or print sizes, electronic or hard copy • ensuring interview notes are kept regarding any support requirements needed and these are communicated to relevant people: for example, dyslexia, epilepsy, diabetes • ensuring students have had access to impartial IAG to consider all their options • ensuring programmes are offered at times everyone can attend • exploring flexible programme delivery or blended learning approaches • finding ways to overcome barriers such as finance, childcare, etc. • removing barriers to enable students to access information, staff, documents and buildings • using initial assessment results to plan individual learning
Planning learning	• agreeing individual learning plans/action plans • creating resources and materials which positively promote all aspects of community and society, equality and diversity • creating schemes of work and session plans to reflect how you will include all students in sessions • differentiating your teaching approaches and activities to address individual differences; for example, levels or speed of learning • ensuring off-site visits are accessible by all: for example, transport and stairs • ensuring the environment is accessible to all students • planning opportunities to develop motivation, self-esteem and confidence within your students • planning your delivery to meet the needs of all learning styles
Facilitating learning	• avoiding favouritism and positive discrimination • being approachable and accessible, enabling your students to feel comfortable to talk to you • being aware that everyone has different experiences, interests, skills and knowledge which will affect their ability to develop and learn • carrying out an icebreaker or energiser which includes everyone • challenging stereotyping, discrimination and prejudice as it happens

Facilitating learning *continued*	<ul><li>drawing on personal experiences of students during each session</li><li>embedding the functional skills of maths, English and ICT</li><li>encouraging group discussions and activities where everyone can participate</li><li>encouraging group work where students can mix and participate with all members of the group over a period of time</li><li>encouraging respect and promoting understanding of student differences</li><li>ensuring students have access to facilities, resources and equipment which is appropriate for the subject and level of learning</li><li>ensuring the language and jargon you use is at an appropriate level</li><li>following up absences and ensuring students have access to any missed material</li><li>identifying where modifications or changes are needed to ensure everyone is felt included</li><li>involving all students within your session, using their names, using eye contact and asking individual questions</li><li>not excluding any student for any reason</li><li>providing a safe and supportive environment where everyone's contribution is valued</li><li>using a wide range of teaching and learning approaches based upon student needs</li></ul>
Assessing learning	<ul><li>adapting assessment activities where possible to meet any particular requirements or needs</li><li>encouraging all students to reach their full potential</li><li>ensuring assessment planning is individual</li><li>giving ongoing developmental feedback at a level to suit the student</li><li>recognising and valuing individual achievements</li></ul>
Quality assurance and Evaluation	<ul><li>communicating with your team members to ensure they are aware of any student requirements or issues</li><li>evaluating your delivery to ensure you have included all students fully in your session</li><li>liaising with the awarding organisation regarding any modifications required to the learning and assessment activities</li><li>obtaining feedback from your students in different ways: for example, verbally, written or electronically</li></ul>

Summary

In this chapter you have learnt about:

- identifying needs of the organisation, teachers and students
- initial and diagnostic assessment
- potential needs of students and points of referral
- equality and diversity
- inclusive learning.

Cross-referencing grid

This chapter contributes towards the following: scope (S), knowledge (K) and practice (P) aspects of the Professional Teaching Standards (A–F domains) and the PTLLS units' assessment criteria. Full details of the learning outcomes and assessment criteria for each PTLLS unit can be found in the appendices.

Domain	Standards
A	ASI, AS2, AS3, AS5, AS6, AS7, AKI.I, AK2.I, AK3.I, AK5.2, API.I, AP2.I, AP2.2, AP3.I, AP5.I, AP5.2, AP6.2
B	BSI, BS3, BS4, BK2.5, BK3.4, BK3.5, BK4.I, BP2.5, BP3.5, BP4.I
C	CK3.2, CK3.5, CP3.2, CP3.3, CP4.2
D	DSI, DS2, DK2.2, DPI.I
E	ESI, ES3, EKI.I, EK2.I
F	FSI, FS2, FS4, FKI.I, FKI.2, FK2.I, FK4.I, FK4.2, FPI.I, FPI.2, FP2.I, FP3.I, FP4.I, FP4.2

PTLLS unit	Assessment criteria	
	Level 3	Level 4
Roles, responsibilities and relationships in lifelong learning	1.2, 1.4 2.2	1.2, 1.4 2.2
Understanding inclusive learning and teaching in lifelong learning	1.3 3.1	1.3 3.1
Using inclusive learning and teaching approaches in lifelong learning	2.1, 2.3	2.1, 2.4
Principles of assessment in lifelong learning		

Theory focus

References and further information

Ayers, H and Gray, F (2006) *An A to Z Practical Guide to Learning Difficulties*. London: David Fulton Publishers.

Clark, T (2010) *Mental Health Matters for FE: Teachers Toolkit*. Leicester: NIACE.

Gravells, A and Simpson, S (2012) *Equality and Diversity in the Lifelong Learning Sector* (2nd edn). Exeter: Learning Matters.

Institute for Learning (2008) *Code of Professional Practice*. London: IfL.

Institute for Learning (2009) *Guidelines for your CPD*. London: IfL.

Race, P (2010) *Making Learning Happen*. London: Sage Publications Ltd.

Websites

Database of self help groups – www.self-help.org.uk

Dyslexia Association – www.dyslexia.uk.net

Equality and Diversity Forum – www.edf.org.uk

Equality and Human Rights Commission – www.equalityhumanrights.com

Open University inclusive practice – www.open.ac.uk/inclusiveteaching/pages/inclusive-teaching/index.php

Support for adult learners – www.direct.gov.uk/adultlearning

4 PLANNING LEARNING

Introduction

In this chapter you will learn about:

- schemes of work and session plans
- differentiation
- resources
- literacy, language and numeracy
- ICT

There are activities and examples to help you reflect on the above which will assist your understanding of how to plan your teaching and learning sessions. At the end of each section is an extension activity to stretch and challenge your learning further.

At the end of the chapter is a cross-referencing grid showing how the chapter's contents contribute towards the professional teaching standards and PTLLS units.

Schemes of work and session plans

To enable effective learning, you need to plan what you are going to teach and when. A scheme of work (sometimes referred to as a learning programme) is a document used to structure the teaching of your subject in a progressive way. It can be for a whole programme or just a unit of a qualification and can be amended at any time if necessary. It should be flexible to allow for any changes – for example, a cancelled session due to adverse weather – and detailed enough in case a colleague needs to cover for you. You will need to prepare one whether you teach groups or individuals. However, you might teach from a scheme of work that someone else has devised rather than having to create your own. If you teach the same subject as your colleagues, you could all work together to produce a standardised scheme of work. This will enable all students to have the same learning experience no matter who their teacher is. If you meet your students for only one session, you will not need a scheme of work, just a session plan. Individual learning plans would be better than a scheme of work if you have students who are all working to different requirements during your sessions.

A session plan is a detailed breakdown of each date on your scheme of work. It will outline all the teaching and learning activities, with allocated timings, assessment activities and resources required. It will also take into account the individual requirements of your students.

Templates or pro-formas for schemes of work and session plans, and the amount of detail you are expected to enter, will vary depending upon the context within which you teach. The requirements of your organisation and external inspectors will also need to be taken into account.

Creating a scheme of work

You will need the syllabus or qualification handbook to ensure you teach and assess all the required content. If none is available, i.e. you are teaching a non-accredited programme, you will need to devise your own programme content, along with suitable delivery and assessment material to meet the needs of your students. When creating your scheme of work, it is useful to know something about your students: for example, their previous knowledge and/or experience, their learning styles or any particular requirements they may have. This will enable you to plan your teaching and learning activities to achieve maximum potential. You might like to put yourself in the place of the student when planning the order of what you will teach. This way you can see things from a beginner's perspective to ensure you keep things simple during the earlier sessions. Because you are a knowledgeable teacher, you might tend to want to achieve too much in the early stages, which could confuse your students, even though it's very clear to you. Always ask yourself what are you going to do with your students and why.

A rationale such as using 'five Ws and one H', *who, what, when, where, why* and *how*, will help you create your scheme of work.

Activity

Consider the five Ws and one H for the subject you will be teaching. Can you obtain all this information easily? What else will you need to know prior to creating your scheme of work? What constraints might you encounter and who can help you if you have any concerns?

A scheme of work will help you create a logical progression of learning and should be based on the five Ws and one H rationale; for example:

- who the sessions are for, and the aim (who and why)
- objectives or learning outcomes (what)

- dates, number of sessions, and venue (when and where)

- activities, resources and assessment (how).

See Table 4.1 on page 65 for a basic example.

There are various aspects you need to consider prior to creating your scheme of work. For example, do you need to:

- obtain a syllabus to enable you to break the content down into a logical order and manageable chunks (remember what must and could be learnt depending upon how much time you have)

- know aspects about your students, e.g. age range, ability, prior knowledge

- obtain any information about the subject or partake in any training yourself

- allow time for an induction, initial assessment, icebreaker and ground rules in the first session

- allow time to check if students have had effective information, advice and guidance

- find out what rooms, facilities and resources are available

- embed literacy, language, numeracy and ICT

- plan activities and materials which can be differentiated and are inclusive

- know the dates and times when students will be attending

- liaise with others

- plan homework activities

- devise delivery and assessment materials

- evaluate the programme delivery and your own performance?

Your scheme of work should show a variety of teaching and learning activities to suit all learning styles. Your sessions should follow in a logical order, which might not be the order printed in the syllabus. Assessment activities should be formative and summative, informal and formal (see Chapter 6).

Make sure you check all dates carefully in case there are any bank, public or religious holidays on the dates you would normally teach. The first session should include an induction to the programme and organisation, an icebreaker and the setting of ground rules (see Chapter 5). You might also need to assess prior learning in this session, or before your students commence. All subsequent sessions should begin with a recap of the previous session and time for questions, and end with an explanation of the next session. The final session should include an evaluation activity to obtain feedback from your students which will help you improve in future, along with details of how students can progress,

Table 4.1 Example – basic scheme of work showing first, second and last sessions

Programme/qualification Introduction to Information Communication Technology Level 1	Group composition 10 adults with little or no previous experience	Dates from: 8 Sept to: 13 Oct
Number of sessions Six	**Contact hours** 18 (3 per week) **Non-contact hours** 2	**Venue** Room 3

Aim of programme To enable students to use a computer (for basic word processing, spreadsheets, database, internet and e-mail)

Dates	Objectives *Students can:*	Activities and resources	Assessment
Week 1 8 Sept	• obtain and discuss information regarding the programme, organisation and assessment • switch on a computer and use a keyboard and mouse • complete an initial assessment to ascertain learning styles • identify previous knowledge/experience and test results • describe and use ICT applications	Induction, icebreaker, ground rules, explanation of programme and organisation, initial assessment, practical and theoretical demonstration and discussion, video, differentiated activities based upon results of learning styles and to meet individual needs, explanation of next session Resources: computers, interactive whiteboard, workpacks, flipchart, handouts, exercises, quiz	Oral questions Initial assessment Observation Discussion
Week 2 15 Sept	• create, save and print documents using a word-processing program	Recap previous session, demonstration of word processing, discussion of uses, differentiated activities and assessments, explanation of next session Resources: computers, interactive whiteboard, workpacks, handouts	Observation Oral and written questions Practical activities Gapped handout
Week 6 13 Oct	• use all programs • carry out an assessment activity • complete an evaluation form • discuss progression opportunities	Recap all sessions, explain and discuss formal assessment process, those not taking will continue with individual exercises. Complete programme evaluation, explain progression opportunities, case study activity Resources: computers, interactive whiteboard, workpacks, exercises, case study, evaluation form, assignments, handout	Formal assignment Observation Questions

i.e. what steps they can take to further their development. You will need to check if you will have the same venue for all the sessions, and what facilities, equipment and resources will be available. The more time you take to plan your scheme of work, the easier it will be to create your session plans and enable learning to be effective.

Aims and objectives

These are terms used to express what you want your students to achieve and how they will go about this. The aim is a broad statement of intent of what you want your students to achieve: for example, *to enable students to use a computer*. The objective is how your students will do this: for example, *switch on a computer and use a keyboard and mouse*.

The term *learning outcomes* might be used instead, depending upon the type of qualification you are teaching: for example, if it is on the QCF Framework.

Always think of the aim as *what* you want your students to achieve, and the objectives as *how* they will achieve it.

Objectives should always be SMART:

- **S**pecific – are they clearly defined?
- **M**easurable – can they be met?
- **A**chievable – are they possible?
- **R**ealistic – are they relevant and relate to the aim?
- **T**ime bound – can target dates/times be met?

SMART objectives enable you to teach and assess learning effectively. Always make sure the words you are using are of the right level for your students, for example *list* is easier than *evaluate*. Objectives should be challenging enough to ensure learning is progressive, and inclusive to all students to ensure they can achieve.

When writing objectives, try not to use the words *know, learn,* or *understand*. These are not SMART and you would find it difficult to assess that learning has taken place.

Example

'Students will state the names of the Kings and Queens of England from 1066 to the present day.'
This is better than:
'Students will know the Kings and Queens of England from 1066 to the present day', and will show you that learning has taken place.

There are two types of objectives: behavioural and non-behavioural which relate to skills and knowledge.

Behavioural – this is when your students can demonstrate a skill: for example, *students will change a fuse in a plug*.

Non-behavioural – this is when your students can demonstrate they have gained knowledge: for example, *students will understand the law of gravity*. Non-behavioural objectives are more difficult to assess and often contain the words *know, learn* or *understand*. If you use non-behavioural objectives, try to make them SMART: for example, *students will understand the law of gravity by explaining how it occurs*. The addition of the word *explaining* enables you to assess that learning has taken place.

Learning outcomes and assessment criteria

Another term widely used in the QCF is *learning outcomes*. These may be longer in terms of time taken for your students to achieve, i.e. they might not achieve them within one session. The word *understand* often appears in the QCF learning outcomes. However, it's the assessment criteria that make them SMART. For an example, look at the learning outcomes and assessment criteria of PTLLS in Appendices 1–8. Although the learning outcomes and assessment criteria will have been written for you, you will still need to use aims and objectives to help you to break down your subject into more manageable topics. Learning outcomes are what *the student will* do and assessment criteria are what *the student can* do.

Domains of learning

Bloom (1956) stated that learning goes through five stages which can affect a person's thinking, emotions and actions. These are known as cognitive, affective, and psycho-motor domains (see Chapter 2). Attention is the first stage, leading through to a change in behaviour once learning has been successful. The stages are:

- attention
- perception
- understanding
- short-/long-term memory
- change in behaviour.

When creating your scheme of work, you need to consider which domain you want to reach.

Example

Teaching historical facts would be the cognitive (thinking) domain.
Discussing the issue of fox hunting would be the affective (emotions) domain.
Demonstrating how to change a washer in a tap would be the psycho-motor
(actions) domain.

Bloom also identified six different levels of learning with associated objectives. These are:

- knowledge – list, recall, state
- comprehension – describe, explain, identify
- application – apply, construct, solve
- analysis – calculate, compare, contrast
- synthesis – argue, define, summarise
- evaluation – criticise, evaluate, reflect.

Using Bloom's theory will help you differentiate the objectives you set to meet the correct level of your students.

Example

Barbara teaches health and safety to a group of 20 students. To test the knowledge
of the full group she asks them to list three important Acts of legislation. To test
comprehension of this legislation, she asks everyone to explain three points of each
Act. Only eight students were able to. Of those eight, she asks how they could apply
the content of the Acts to a real working situation. Only two students were able to.
This shows Barbara what level her students are at, enabling her to differentiate the
teaching and learning approaches accordingly.

Tables 4.2 and 4.3 opposite give examples of objectives you could use to help plan your sessions. Always be careful to choose the right objective for the level of your students: for example, *to list* is easier than *to analyse*.

Creating a session plan

A session plan should be produced prior to teaching and relate to your scheme of work. Although it's very similar to the scheme of work, it is much more detailed and helps you manage the time that you are with your students. You need to consider what you want your students to be able to know or do by the end of the session, i.e. your aim. SMART objectives will help you focus on this and enable you to see that learning has taken place. Try not to prepare too many session plans in advance, as circumstances may change and you want the

Table 4.2 SMART objectives

• analyse	• describe	• practise
• answer	• design	• present
• assemble	• differentiate	• print
• build	• draw	• produce
• calculate	• estimate	• recall
• carry out	• explain	• recap
• change	• identify	• recognise
• choose	• illustrate	• repeat
• clarify	• justify	• select
• classify	• label	• show
• compare	• list	• sing
• complete	• make	• sketch
• construct	• measure	• solve
• contrast	• name	• state
• convert	• obtain	• summarise
• cook	• operate	• switch
• create	• organise	• use
• define	• participate	• weigh
• demonstrate	• perform	• write

Table 4.3 Objectives which are not SMART and therefore more difficult to assess

• accept	• establish	• plan
• adapt	• evaluate	• praise
• adopt	• explore	• prepare
• allow	• facilitate	• provide
• apply	• familiarise	• question
• appreciate	• formulate	• rationalise
• assist	• gain	• read
• attempt	• hear	• reflect
• be aware of	• help	• relate
• believe	• interpret	• review
• challenge	• introduce	• save
• criticise	• join	• see
• defend	• judge	• share
• develop	• know	• study
• devise	• learn	• suggest
• discuss	• listen	• support
• dispute	• look	• understand
• enable	• maintain	• visualise
• encourage	• manage	• volunteer
• enjoy	• outline	• watch

information to be fresh in your mind. Once you have a set of session plans, you can adapt them in the future for different groups of students, rather than starting again.

Each plan should have an introduction, development and conclusion/summary; in other words, a beginning, middle, and end, with times allocated to the activities within each. Your introduction should include the aim of the session and a recap of the previous session (if applicable). This should hopefully arouse interest and link to previous learning. You could carry out a starter activity to gain attention and focus learning, for example, a short quiz. If this is your first meeting with your students, make sure you introduce yourself, explain the facilities of the organisation, the requirements of the programme, carry out an icebreaker and agree the ground rules. You can also carry out any practical matters such as taking the register, or reminding students of any important issues.

The development stage is where teaching and learning should take place and should be in a logical sequence for learning to progress. Imagine you are teaching someone to make a cup of tea. You can probably do it without thinking; however, for a student who hasn't done it before you need to appreciate just how many steps are involved. It's the same with your subject: you know it well, but for a new student you need to break it down into smaller logical steps. You should include a variety of theory and practical approaches, activities and assessments to help maintain motivation and interest. You need to engage and include your students by asking questions, holding discussions and carrying out activities. If you don't vary your activities the students may become bored, lose concentration or be disruptive. Try to use 70 per cent of the session for student activities and 30 per cent for teaching activities.

Don't expect too much from your students at first; they don't know what you know and will need time to assimilate new knowledge and skills. Don't forget to allow time for a break if necessary. Before concluding your session, you might like to ask questions to check knowledge (one aimed at each student if you have time). If you have a large group, you could split them into teams and ask questions in the form of a quiz. This is a fun way of ending the session and shows you how much learning has taken place.

Your conclusion should include a summary of your original aim and relate to the objectives which have been achieved. You should allow time for any questions and to discuss any homework or other issues. You can then state what the aim of your next session will be (if applicable).

Be prepared – better to have too much than not enough. Unused material can be carried forward to another session or given as homework. Also, consider students who may finish tasks early: can you give them something else to do?

You should always evaluate your session; this could be afterwards when you have time to reflect, and/or by making notes as you progress, i.e. if something didn't work well you could put a cross next to it on your session plan. You could note your strengths, areas for development and any action and improvements required for the future. Your plan may even change as you progress through your session to take into account the needs of your students.

See Table 4.4 on page 72 for a basic example of a session plan and see how the objectives are SMART.

There are a number of aspects to consider when creating your session plan.

- The overall aim – what you expect your students to achieve during this session.
- Group composition – details of individual students and needs to enable differentiation to take place.
- Objectives – how your students will achieve your aim – how do they link to the syllabus, what order will you teach them, what timings will you allocate to each? Remember to include breaks if applicable.
- Resources – what you need to effectively teach your session – do you need to check or book anything in advance? Do you have a contingency plan?
- Teacher activities – what you will be doing. Use a variety of theory and practical approaches to meet all learning styles.
- Student activities – what your students will be doing and for how long – how will you keep them motivated? How will you ensure inclusion of all students and differentiation? Do you have spare activities in case some students finish before others? What could you remove if you run out of time?
- Assessment – how will you assess that learning has taken place?
- The next session – how will you link the sessions?

Activity

Watch one of the main news programmes on television. Notice how the presenters introduce the stories, then explain them in more detail and recap them at the end. Often there are two presenters, one male and one female, the camera shots change and there are videos and pictures to back up the stories. They will have planned and prepared well, having a contingency plan in case anything goes wrong. Did you take into account what the presenters look like and what they were wearing? Did this distract you in any way from the news?

Table 4.4 Example – basic session plan for the first session from the scheme of work

Teacher	A N Other	Date	8 September	Venue	Room 3
Subject/level Syllabus ref	Introduction to Information Communication Technology Level I Ref I.I	**Time and duration**	6–9 p.m.	**Number of students**	10
Aim of session	To induct students to the programme, organisation and assessment requirements To enable students to use a computer				
Group composition	10 adults with little or no previous experience of computers (4 female, 6 male) Initial assessment during this session will identify any prior knowledge and learning styles. One student is dyslexic and requires handouts on pastel coloured paper. All students will complete all planned activities, most will complete a gapped handout and some will complete an additional activity if they finish early.				

Timing	Objectives Students can:	Resources	Teacher activities	Student activities	Assessment
6.00	Obtain and discuss information regarding the programme, organisation and assessment requirements	Handouts Flipchart and paper Interactive board	Explanation and discussion	Gain knowledge Listen and ask questions	Oral questions
6.20	Complete an icebreaker	Handout	Facilitate icebreaker	Partake in icebreaker	Observation
6.40	State ground rules	Flipchart	Facilitate ground rules	Discuss ground rules	Discussion
6.50	Switch on a computer and use a keyboard and mouse	Computers Workpacks Exercises Interactive board	Practical demonstration	Observe teacher Use keyboard and mouse	Oral questions
(7.30 Break)					
7.45	Complete an initial assessment to ascertain learning styles	Computers (online test)	Facilitate initial assessment	Complete initial assessment and learning styles test	Observation Test
8.15	Identify previous knowledge/ experience and test results	Printed test results	Discussion	Discussion	Oral questions
8.25	Describe and use ICT applications	Interactive board (connected to internet)	Show video Facilitate practical activities	View video Use sample programs Complete gapped handout	Oral questions Observation Gapped handout
8.55	Switch off computers	Flipchart	Summarise session Explain next session	Log off Hear a summary of the session Ask questions	Oral questions
9.00 End	Tidy work area and leave		Ensure computers off		

Newsreaders have an autocue to read from; they also have the news written in paper format as a contingency plan in case anything goes wrong. They will have a script which shows the timings for the news stories and who will read them, rather like a session plan.

Your session plan should be visible at all times for you to refer to and to check how your timings are progressing. You may need to remove an activity if you are overrunning, or add something if you have spare time. You could highlight key words on your session plan to quickly glance at to help you remain focused. Or you could prepare cue cards – small pieces of card with key words or statements on that you hold in your hand or have visible close by. These will act as prompts, particularly if you have a lot of complex information to remember.

Extension Activity

Create a scheme of work for six sessions in your subject area. You may need to obtain a syllabus first; you can decide the length of each session. Create the first two session plans. Now reflect upon how easy or difficult this was, and what information you needed but couldn't obtain. How will this knowledge help you improve your planning skills and meet the individual needs of your students?

Differentiation

Differentiation is about using a range of different approaches and resources to meet the needs of individuals and groups. It is very rare that a teacher has a group of students who are all at the same level of ability, with the same prior knowledge and experience, who have the same needs. You don't have to individualise everything you do, you just need to take individual needs into account: for example, their learning styles. You wouldn't help your students if you delivered a theoretical session to a practical group of students. Small group work is a good way to use differentiation. You could group your students for different activities by their learning style, level of ability, level of qualification or assessment criteria, past experiences or current knowledge, etc.

> *Differentiation can be defined as an approach to teaching and learning that both recognises the individuality of learners and also informs ways of planning for learning and teaching that take these individualities into consideration.*
>
> (Tummons, 2010, page 93)

You could plan different activities which *all* your students are capable of achieving, as well as what *most* or *some* can achieve according to their level and ability.

Example

Paul has a mixed group of level 2 and 3 students taking a Certificate in Customer Service. He knows the full group will be able to answer questions based on the level 2 syllabus, most will be able to answer from both levels and some will be able to answer questions based on the level 3 syllabus. He has therefore devised and used a differentiated questioning technique for his group of students.

A dyslexic student may prefer to work with more images, have handouts printed on pastel coloured paper, wish to make an audio recording of the session to listen to afterwards or key in notes directly to a laptop. An older student might shy away from using new technology whereas younger students may expect to access and use it. Differentiated questioning can help support students; for example, students for whom English is a second language may need longer to process information or need questions rephrasing. Acknowledging and embracing the diverse nature of your students' age, experience, culture and background should help you include all students and bring your subject to life. Some students may work quicker than others; giving them an extension activity could help develop and challenge their learning further, without compromising the learning of others.

Initial assessment is crucial to gain the information you need to plan effectively; however, not all your students may reveal things during the application process or on formal documentation. If you can encourage your students to let you know of anything that you can do to help them, you will improve their learning experience. Simply asking, *Is there anything I can do to help your learning?* should ascertain this. Alternatively, ask yourself *What can I do to give everyone a good learning experience?*

Differentiating your teaching, learning and assessment approaches should lead to more confident students who feel included, are motivated to learn and able to achieve. While it may take longer to plan and prepare your sessions to differentiate effectively, you will find your students are more engaged and motivated rather than being bored and uninterested.

Extension Activity

What will you need to know about your students to plan for effective differentiation of teaching, learning and assessment? Will this affect the initial assessment procedure? How can you differentiate the objectives and resources to take into account the needs of your students?

Resources

Resources are all the aids, books, handouts, items of equipment, objects and people that you can use to deliver and assess your subject. They should stimulate learning, add impact and promote interest in the subject. Resources should be accessible and inclusive to all students, while enabling them to acquire new skills and knowledge. When using or creating resources, ensure they promote equality of opportunity, reflect diversity and challenge stereotypes. For example, text and pictures in a handout should portray all aspects of society. Resources should be appropriate in terms of level, quality, quantity and content and be relevant to the subject and the learning expected. Handouts and presentations should be checked for spelling, grammar, punctuation and sentence construction errors. You could put your name, date and organisation details on any documents to show where they originated. You may also find it useful to add a file name and version number to keep track of any changes.

If you give a handout at the beginning of the session, you may find your students fiddle with it and become distracted. If you can, issue handouts at an appropriate time and talk through the content, asking questions to ensure your students have understood. Otherwise, issue them at the end of the session and ask students to read them at home to help reinforce what has been covered during the session. Alternatively, to aid sustainability, you could upload handouts to a VLE or e-mail them to your students. Handouts can also be used as activities; for example, a gapped handout can contain sentences with missing words that students need to fill in. These are useful to test lower-level students, as a fun team activity or to fill in time at the end of a session. If a resource you are using is not effective with some students, try changing the experience rather than the resource. You might need to explain the resource differently or change a group activity to become an individual one.

Examples of resources include:

- audio/visual equipment
- books, catalogues, journals, magazines
- computerised presentations
- Information Communication Technology
- digital cameras
- flipchart paper and pens
- handouts
- interactive or electronic whiteboards
- people: specialist speakers, colleagues
- physical resources, models and apparatus
- projector
- radios/televisions
- textbooks
- worksheets, puzzles or crosswords.

Depending upon your subject and what is available, you may need to create your own or adapt someone else's resources. This could be a handout of useful information, an exercise, activity or worksheet or it could be a complex working model used to demonstrate a topic. If you can search the internet, you might find resources for your subject area are freely available. Whatever resources you use, it's important to ensure they cover all learning styles and meet the differing needs of your students. Putting posters on the wall of the room will help to reinforce points. Students may not always look at them consciously, but subconsciously will glance at them, taking in the information. You might have to acknowledge your organisation's resource constraints and make best use of what is available. You should always evaluate the effectiveness of any resources you use, to modify or change them for future use.

When designing resources, any individual needs should be taken into account: for example, dyslexia, hearing impairment, sight impairment, physical or mental disabilities. You may need to produce handouts in a larger-sized font, on different coloured paper, or ensure there is plenty of white space surrounding the text. White space is blank space on the page. You also need to consider the location, cost, challenges and benefits of using certain resources. If you are using, adapting or copying work, you will need to check you are not in breach of copyright. Using pictures as well as text and not putting too much information on a handout will help learning. If you were given one handout with a lot of written information in small text, and another with text in a larger more pleasing font with a few pictures, which one would you prefer to read? It would probably be the latter.

You may have to deal with unexpected situations which relate to resources. It is useful to have a contingency plan just in case.

Example

Jack was due to deliver a food hygiene session to a group of 12 students at 7 p.m. He had created a computerised presentation and saved it to a memory stick. He arrived at the venue half an hour early, only to find a notice on the door stating he had been moved to another room. In the other room were two circular tables that would seat six students comfortably, but only four chairs at each. He switched on the computer and realised the version of his presentation was newer than the one on the computer and wouldn't open. If he didn't have a contingency plan he would have been unable to deliver the session. However, because he was early he was able to locate and ask the caretaker to bring four extra chairs. He had printouts of the presentation which he could hand out to each student, but had time to go to the office and resave the document in a previous version. While there, he saved it to the organisation's hard drive which was accessible from any room, just in case a problem occurred with his memory stick.

Preparing for unforeseen circumstances comes with experience. Whenever you are due to teach a session, ask yourself, *What would I do if something wasn't available or doesn't work?* You might prepare a computerised presentation and make copies as handouts that you can give your students. However, if you can't get copies made in time, you can still deliver your presentation and offer to e-mail a copy to your students, upload it to a VLE, or get photocopies made later. Try not to rely totally on presentation software when teaching: use different approaches and activities to add variety.

Evaluating resources

You should always evaluate the resources you use to improve or amend them for future use. It could be that a handout you used with your students was not read thoroughly, for example there was too much text on it or they found it too complex. Or it could be you have used a working model to demonstrate something but it didn't function on the day. Always practise with your resources in advance of using them with your students, just in case anything could go wrong.

What works with one student or group might not work well with others, perhaps due to their learning styles or other influences. Don't change something for the sake of it; if it works, hopefully it will continue to work.

When evaluating the resources you have used, ask yourself the following.

- Did the resource do what I expected? If not why not?
- Did it support and reinforce learning effectively?
- Did it reach all learning styles, i.e. was there something to look at (visual), did I talk about it and could students discuss it (aural), was there something written and/or could students make notes (read/write), was there something practical for students to do (kinaesthetic)?
- Were all students able to use it with ease and was there enough for everyone?
- Did it motivate the students to learn more?
- Was it up to date and relevant to the subject?
- Was it active or passive? Do my students prefer to be actively engaged when using resources, such as a working model rather than passively reading a handout?
- Was it easy for me to create? Can I update it easily?
- Did I encounter any problems setting it up and using it? Was it too time consuming?

- Did I carry out any necessary risk assessments?
- Was it of high quality and professional looking?

After evaluating your resource, you can make any necessary changes before using it again. Don't forget to ask for feedback from your students as they are best able to inform you how effective it was.

Extension Activity

What resources could you use during your sessions to ensure both teaching and learning are effective for your subject? Review the advantages and limitations of these. Do you need to produce any resources yourself, or are there some already available you could use or adapt? Use an appropriate resource during one of your sessions and evaluate its effectiveness. If you don't know how to use the resources at your organisation ask for a training session.

Literacy, language and numeracy

Wherever possible, you should try and improve the literacy, language and numeracy skills of your students. These terms have had many labels such as Basic Skills, Skills for Life, Key Skills, Core Skills, Essential Skills and Functional Skills. In 2007 as part of the reform of 14–19 and adult education, Functional Skills were introduced as a pilot by the Labour Government. This was to equip the United Kingdom with the skills it needs for the 21st century. Functional Skills consist of English, maths and ICT and are currently taken by apprentice students. They provide the essential knowledge, skills and understanding that will enable people to function confidently, effectively and independently in life and at work. You might be required to embed the three Functional Skills within your sessions, and/or help improve the literacy, language and numeracy skills of your students, for example:

- English or literacy and language – reading, writing, listening, speaking, discussing
- maths or numeracy – approximations, estimations, calculations, measurements.

If possible, you should also embed ICT skills to help your students improve, for example:

- ICT – e-mail, web-based research, word-processing assignments and reports, using spreadsheets, databases and presentation packages.

To help improve the literacy, language and numeracy of your own students, you could use subtle activities so they don't realise they are learning these skills.

Example

Sanjay is due to teach Cookery for Beginners and plans to improve his students' skills as follows:

- *literacy – discussing recipes, talking, listening and asking questions*
- *language – reading recipes, researching and reading healthy eating websites, writing a list of ingredients, word processing a menu*
- *numeracy – calculating weights and costs of ingredients, measuring amounts, estimating calorific values, cooking times and temperatures.*

You might feel your own skills in these areas need improving therefore you could partake in further training yourself. If you are not competent you will not set a good example to your students. For example, if you spell words wrongly in a handout, have difficulty making calculations or can't use a computer, your students may lose confidence in you as a teacher. If you are progressing to a further teaching qualification after the PTLLS Award and wish to gain your teaching status, you will be required to prove your own skills to at least level 2. This is known as the Minimum Core in literacy, language, numeracy and ICT.

When teaching, it's best to find naturally occurring opportunities whenever possible as this will enable your students to see it as part of the subject, not as a separate lesson. Students who possess good literacy, language and numeracy skills should be able to progress in education, training and employment and make a positive contribution to the communities in which they live and work.

Example

Ravi teaches plumbing in a realistic working environment, and has realised that many aspects of the job naturally include the use of literacy, language and numeracy skills. Talking to customers and suppliers, reading manuals and writing orders all involve literacy and language. Measuring pipes, calculating the amount of materials to use and working out invoices all involve numeracy skills. Ravi also encourages his students to use ICT by researching materials on the internet, e-mailing suppliers and maintaining an electronic diary.

When embedding the skills during sessions, they must be realistic and relevant to enable your students to engage with real situations in their subject area. You can also encourage your students to carry out activities in their own time to help them improve their skills. There might be free courses in your area or via the internet that students could take. If there are library facilities locally you could give your students an activity to carry out some research. They could produce a short presentation, individually or in groups, and report back on their findings. If you upload materials to a VLE, your students could access these to read at a later date, amend them to an appropriate font or size, and save or print if they wish to access them again.

Extension Activity

How could you provide opportunities for your students to practise their literacy, language, numeracy and ICT skills? Design an activity to incorporate some or all of the skills, try it out and then evaluate how effective it was. Ask your students if they realised they were learning these skills along with the subject.

Information and communication technology

ICT should be used whenever possible during teaching and learning to engage and stimulate your students. It will also help raise their confidence if they haven't used ICT much in the past. You might deliver and assess your subject via an online program or use a blended approach of traditional teaching supported with access to technology. ICT can encompass a wide variety of activities besides using computers or accessing the internet; for example:

- audio and video clips (creating or viewing)
- calculators
- computer programs
- digital cameras, camcorders and video recorders
- e-assessments
- electronic brain games
- electronic templates
- e-mail
- e-portfolios and e-assessment
- interactive and online programs
- mobile and smart phones
- online discussions
- presentation packages
- scanners
- social networking (if appropriate)
- video conferencing
- VLEs
- webcast, weblog, short messages, podcast, etc.

You would need to feel confident using ICT equipment yourself and may therefore need further training. You would also need to ensure everything is accessible, in working order and appropriate for your students.

> *Some 42 per cent of adult learners most like to learn by doing practical things, a figure that is unchanged since 1998. However, now almost a quarter (23 per cent) mentioned using computers, mobile phones and the internet, not feasible options for most in 1998.*
>
> (Campaign for Learning, 2009)

When using ICT, remember to vary your methods to reach different learning styles and address individual needs. Technology can help overcome barriers to learning; for example, pairing an experienced student with an inexperienced student so that someone who hasn't used it before doesn't feel alone. You also need to be careful that students are using it appropriately, i.e. not accessing unsuitable websites or checking their e-mails while you think they are working. Some students may be concerned about using ICT; for example, a student with epilepsy may need regular breaks from a computer screen. You could let your students bring laptops or tablets to use for writing notes rather than pen or paper.

You might use equipment such as an interactive or electronic whiteboard. With a normal whiteboard, once you have written on it, you need to clean it before using it again. With the interactive whiteboard, you use a special pen directly onto the board, information is displayed and can be transferred to a computer for saving, printing, uploading to a VLE and/or e-mailing. You can open documents, move between pages and add text and pictures, link to the internet and show video clips. You can involve your students by getting them to use it to create and use documents, quizzes, pictures, presentations, etc.

Example

Angela is teaching a new group of students how to use a computer. She is able to demonstrate how to use various functions by displaying each program on the interactive whiteboard, enabling everyone to see what she does. Previously, she would have had to gather the group around one small computer screen. She can also link to the internet to demonstrate how to use e-mail and access websites.

Other equipment you could use includes specialist software for delivering presentations. This would enable you to use graphics as well as text to make your presentation more visual. You can prepare your presentation in advance and save it to a disk, memory stick and/or upload it to a VLE or accessible site. Therefore as long as a computer and data projector are available, you can teach in any room. A wireless remote control is useful as it enables you to move around the room rather than stand next to the keyboard to move the slides. Always have a contingency plan in case anything doesn't work, i.e. an activity students can carry out while you resolve the situation.

Hints for using handouts and presentations

Handouts and presentations are useful resources to add variety to your session and focus attention. You should always check the spelling, grammar and punctuation of any materials you use, otherwise you could come across as unprofessional. If a student does see an error, don't make excuses but thank them and say you will make the changes for future use. Hard copies of your materials will enable your students to refer to them during and after the session to go over important points. However, you might not always be able to get them copied in time. You could consider uploading handouts and presentations to an intranet or VLE to aid sustainability. That way, your students can access, save and print them in a format to suit, for example in a larger font or on coloured paper. Learning doesn't stop just because the session has.

The following are some hints which you could refer to when creating handouts and presentations.

Handouts

- Make the text easily readable, in an appropriate font and size. Don't put too much text or too many pictures on one page and don't mix fancy fonts. It might look good to you, but might not be easily readable by your students. Keep plenty of *white space* (the blank area around the text/pictures). This makes the information stand out clearly and will allow your students to make notes if necessary. If there is too much on a handout your students may find it difficult to read and absorb all the information.

- A single sheet, one sided or double sided, is best; too many pages will take too long for your students to read and assimilate the information. If you do use more pages, always staple in the top left corner and number each page.

- If you have created the handout yourself, type your name, filename, version number and date as a footer. This will enable you to access it easily to make future changes and ensure you are using the most recent version.

- Make sure the information is up to date. You may need to revise something if there have been changes to your subject.

- Consider numbering paragraphs or using numbers instead of bullet points. That way you can direct your students to important points.

- If you have a dyslexic student who would prefer handouts on pastel paper, use the same colour for everyone so that no one is singled out.

- If you are issuing several handouts during a session, you could print them on different coloured paper for ease of reference when you are talking about their content.

- If you use pictures of people, make sure they represent all aspects of society.

- If you use any quotes, make sure you reference them correctly. A list of relevant references or websites is useful to encourage your students to research further.

- Handouts can be useful if incorporated into an activity, for example a gapped handout containing sentences with missing words for students to complete.

- If possible, give handouts towards the end of the activity they refer to. If you give them too early, your students may fiddle with them and read through them rather than concentrating on you.

Presentations

- Always check the equipment and projector are connected and working. As a backup, have your presentation stored to an external drive as well as the internal one. Check that the program and version in which you have saved your presentation is compatible with the one to be used.

- Don't include too much text or use fancy fonts, colours and animations as this could distract from the points you want to make.

- Check if you need to insert a logo on each slide as a footer, or use a particular font and size for consistency throughout the organisation.

- Large, bold plain fonts are easier to read than smaller type, for example **Arial, Comic Sans** or **Verdana**. Serif and script fonts are thought to be more difficult to read, for example **Times New Roman** and *Brush Script*. The font size should be minimum 36 and should be readable from the back of the room. Using combined upper and lower case is preferable to using all upper case as the latter can appear as though you are shouting.

- Blue-eyed people often struggle to see red, orange or yellow text, particularly if on a coloured background. Red and green can cause confusion for students who are colour blind. Be consistent, for example use black text on a white background. Check which colours your students prefer. How you see the colours on the slides may be very different to how your students will see them.

- Use bullet points, three or four per slide, and don't read them verbatim. Schedule them to come in line by line otherwise your students will be reading ahead. Expand on each point and discuss it with your students. Involve them where possible by asking open questions to make the presentation a two-way process.

- Handouts can be given out during a presentation to give further information regarding important points. It's better to have further details on a supporting handout than squashed into a slide.

- Graphs and diagrams are often easier for students to understand than tables; however, don't make them too complex. It's better to use several slides rather than one to express the information.

- If you have time, incorporate a short video to bring your topic to life. If you are connected to the internet you can insert the website link into your slide for easy access.

- If you need to refer to the same slide more than once, copy it rather than moving back through your presentation. Otherwise you could use your place.

- Use a remote control for moving through your slides. This enables you to move around the room rather than standing next to the keyboard.

- Press the letter B on the keyboard to black out the screen, or W to white out, for example if you don't want it on display for a few minutes. Pressing B or W again will restore it.

- If your presentation is given via an electronic whiteboard, you could use features such as writing on the slides with the special pen. You can then save and e-mail it to your students, or upload it to a VLE.

- Involve your students; ask them to use the presentation equipment and/or electronic whiteboard whenever possible.

- Don't rely on using presentations; vary your delivery by using other types of equipment, and teaching and learning approaches.

- Have a hard copy of the presentation for yourself in case something goes wrong. You can then refer to it rather than having nothing.

- If you want your students to make notes throughout the presentation, you can print a copy using the *handout* function. That way, they can have several slides on one A4 page with room for making notes. Printing one slide per A4 sheet is just a waste of paper. If you are not sure how to do this, ask someone to show you.

Online teaching and learning

Lots of programmes are now delivered online, i.e. where students access a programme of learning via a specialist website. This is ideal for students who might have difficulty attending a formal programme, or wish to learn at times convenient to them. Students will need a computer with a reliable internet connection; however, this could be in a library or another suitable location rather than at home.

Teaching and learning can be synchronous (where both teacher and student are online at the same time) and/or asynchronous (where the teacher and student are not online at the same time).

Some programmes are taught purely online, in which case the teacher may never meet their students. Other programmes use a blended approach with some aspects carried out online and others in a training environment. Online programmes can be individual or group based, and usually allow the students to progress at their own pace. Aspects such as icebreakers and ground rules should still be carried out with students to agree boundaries within which to work.

Technology is advancing rapidly where online teaching and learning is concerned. Unfortunately, there isn't room in this book to explain it in detail, therefore please refer to other appropriate texts such as Hill (2008) and others listed at the end of this chapter.

Extension Activity

What ICT resources could you use within your subject? Research new and emerging technologies and create an ICT activity to use with your students. Use the activity and then evaluate its effectiveness. If you are not yet confident with ICT, find out where you could receive training or support.

Summary

In this chapter you have learnt about:

- schemes of work and session plans
- differentiation
- resources
- literacy, language and numeracy
- ICT.

Cross-referencing grid

This chapter contributes towards the following: scope (S), knowledge (K) and practice (P) aspects of the Professional Teaching Standards (A–F domains) and the PTLLS units' assessment criteria. Full details of the learning outcomes and assessment criteria for each PTLLS unit can be found in the appendices.

Domain	Standards
A	ASI, AS2, AS3, AS4, AK3.I, AP3.I
B	BS5, BK2.I, BK2.2, BK2.4, BK5.I, BK5.2, BP2.I, BP5.I, BP5.2
C	CSI, CK3.3, CK3.4, CK3.5, CK4.I, CK4.2, CP3.4, CP3.5
D	DSI, DKI.I, DKI.2, DKI.3, DK2.I, DK2.2, DPI.I, DPI.2, DPI.3, DP2.I, DP2.2, DP3.I
E	
F	

PTLLS unit	Assessment criteria	
	Level 3	**Level 4**
Roles, responsibilities and relationships in lifelong learning		
Understanding inclusive learning and teaching in lifelong learning	I.I 2.I, 2.2, 2.4	I.I 2.I, 2.2, 2.4
Using inclusive learning and teaching approaches in lifelong learning	I.I, I.2 2.2	I.I, I.2 2.2
Principles of assessment in lifelong learning		

Theory focus

References and further information

Becta (2009) *Harnessing Technology Review 2008: The Role of Technology and its Impact on Education*. Coventry: Becta.

Bloom, BS (1956) *Taxonomy of Educational Objectives: Handbook 1*. New York: Longman.

Campaign for Learning (2009) *State of the Nation Survey 2008*. London: Campaign for Learning.

Gravells, A and Simpson, S (2010) *Planning and Enabling Learning in the Lifelong Learning Sector* (2nd edn). Exeter: Learning Matters.

Hill, C (2008) *Teaching with E-learning in the Lifelong Learning Sector* (2nd edn). Exeter: Learning Matters.

Rae, P and Pickford, R (2007) *Making Teaching Work*. London: Sage Publications Ltd.

Tummons, J (2010) *Becoming a Professional Tutor in the Lifelong Learning Sector* (2nd edn). Exeter: Learning Matters.

Wallace, S (2010) *Teaching, Tutoring and Training in the Lifelong Learning Sector* (4th edn). Exeter: Learning Matters.

Websites

Copyright – www.copyrightservice.co.uk

Dyslexia Association – www.dyslexia.uk.net

English and Maths free support – www.move-on.org.uk

ICT free support – www.onlinebasics.co.uk and http://learn.go-on.co.uk

Minimum Core shortcut – http://tinyurl.com/3l5rhvl

National Institute of Adult Continuing Education promoting adult learning – www.niace.org.uk

Qualifications and Credit Framework – http://tinyurl.com/447bgy2

Introduction

In this chapter you will learn about:

- induction, icebreakers and ground rules
- teaching and learning approaches
- communication, behaviour and respect
- working with groups and individuals
- safeguarding and Every Child Matters

There are activities and examples to help you reflect on the above which will assist your understanding of how to teach and enable learning to take place. At the end of each section is an extension activity to stretch and challenge your learning further.

At the end of the chapter is a cross-referencing grid showing how the chapter's contents contribute towards the professional teaching standards and PTLLS units.

Induction, icebreakers and ground rules

When you begin teaching a new group or an individual, there are certain points you must explain regarding your organisation, the programme/subject and the facilities available. This is known as an induction and will usually take place during the first meeting with your students. Carrying out an icebreaker with your students will help ensure they get to know each other and you. Establishing ground rules with your students will help underpin appropriate behaviour and respect throughout their time on the programme.

Induction

Your organisation may have a checklist of general points for you to follow and you may need to add specific points regarding your subject and the learning environment.

It should include aspects such as:

- introducing yourself

- dates and times of attendance

- break times and refreshment facilities

- checking your students have received IAG

- qualification content and assessment requirements

- a tour of the site including location of study areas, learning resources, toilets, catering venues, parking, smoking areas, etc.

- organisational polices such as health and safety, equality and diversity, appeals and complaints

- organisational procedures such as fire and accidents

- an icebreaker to introduce students to each other

- ground rules.

There may be some administrative aspects to be completed during the first session. Don't let this take over – your students will want to leave having learnt something interesting about the subject. If you do have a lot of information and paperwork to complete, inform your students in advance that the first session will be the induction session, and they will not be commencing the subject until the second session. If you have any students who commence the programme at a later date, make sure you spend time with them to cover all aspects of the induction process and introduce them to the other students.

Activity

Imagine you are to begin teaching your subject to a new group of students. Devise a checklist of the information you would need to cover. You could think back to when you started a new programme, i.e. the information you received and the questions you asked. If you are currently teaching, obtain a copy of your organisation's checklist and compare it with yours.

Giving your students a copy of the induction checklist will act as a reminder to them of the information they have received. Often, so much information is given out during the first session that students can easily forget some important points.

Icebreakers

Students can be quiet, shy, nervous or apprehensive when they commence. Carrying out an icebreaker is a good way of everyone getting to know each other's name and encouraging communication to take place. Some students may already know each other, or have carried out an icebreaker with another teacher they currently have. Knowing this beforehand will help you decide upon an appropriate and suitable icebreaker to carry out, and saves repetition. You could carry out the icebreaker before covering the induction requirements as this will encourage your students to relax, and give them confidence to speak or ask questions in front of others.

Icebreakers can be quite simple: for example, asking your students to introduce themselves in front of the group. However, this can be a bit intimidating if none of the students have met before. A way round this is to form the group into pairs and ask them to talk to each other for five minutes about their hobbies, interests and reason for being there. They may find they have something in common and create a bond. You can then ask each person to introduce the person they have been talking to. People may not feel comfortable talking about themselves to a group of strangers, so another person introducing them takes this anxiety away. A good idea is to note down your students' names when they introduce each other, on a rough sketch of a seating plan. This will help you remember their names as it's likely they will return to the same position at the next session. You could also note something about them which you could use in a future conversation. This shows that you are taking an interest in each student as an individual.

If you don't have time for introductions, you could issue name badges for students to wear or name cards to place in front of them. This is a visual reminder to others, and helps you remember and use their name when speaking to them. Always introduce yourself first otherwise students may be wondering what your name is, or whether you are their permanent teacher or just someone facilitating the icebreaker. First impressions count, therefore you need to portray that you are a professional, knowledgeable teacher who is competent and approachable.

More complex icebreakers can involve games or activities, but the outcome should be for your students to relax, enjoy the activity, communicate and ascertain each other's names. Icebreakers help retain attention, keep motivation high and help the group to work together. All students should be included and you should manage the activity carefully to ensure everyone can actively take part. You may wish to include yourself in the icebreaker, or just observe what is happening. If you include yourself, don't get too personal, resist the temptation to be everyone's friend and remain professional throughout.

Icebreakers can also be used during an established session, perhaps after a break to help students refocus. These are called energisers and can be subject-specific such as a quiz or a fun activity or game which gets students moving about. Always have a contingency plan in case anything you planned to use isn't available, or if some students finish before others.

Whichever way you use an icebreaker or an energiser, it should be designed to be a fun and light-hearted activity to:

- break down barriers

- build confidence

- create a suitable learning environment

- enable students to talk confidently in front of their peers

- encourage communication, motivation, interaction, teamwork and inclusion

- establish trust

- get the programme off to a good start

- help students relax

- introduce students to each other

- reduce apprehension and nervousness

- reduce intimidation.

Activity

Imagine you have a new group of 16 students starting next week who have never met before. What sort of icebreaker would you carry out with them and why?

Your organisation may have icebreakers for you to use or you could design your own or search the internet for ideas. Keep your icebreaker short and simple and always evaluate how it went to enable you to modify or improve it for the future.

Ground rules

Ground rules are boundaries, rules and conditions within which students can safely work and learn. They should underpin appropriate behaviour and respect for everyone in the group, including the teacher, and ensure the session runs smoothly. If they are not set, problems may occur which could disrupt the session and lead to misunderstandings or behaviour problems. It is best to agree the ground rules during the first session, perhaps after the icebreaker once everyone is feeling more relaxed.

Ground rules should always be discussed and negotiated with your students rather than forced upon them. Using an activity to do this will help students feel included, take ownership of and hopefully follow the rules. Some ground rules might be renegotiated or added to throughout the programme: for example, changing the break time. Others might not be negotiable but imposed: for example, health and safety requirements. These may already be listed in a student handbook, agreement or student contract and you would need to ensure all students have a copy, and know that they are in addition to any rules agreed as a group.

When establishing ground rules, you need to have an idea of what needs to be imposed and what could be negotiated.

Example

Imposed ground rules:

- *no smoking*
- *arriving on time and returning from breaks punctually*
- *no anti-social behaviour, offensive language or swearing*
- *respecting others' views and beliefs*
- *following health and safety regulations*
- *handing in work on time*
- *not interrupting when someone else is speaking*
- *paying attention and fully participating*
- *leaving the area tidy.*

Negotiable ground rules:

- *no eating or drinking during sessions*
- *standard of dress*
- *switching off mobile phones and electronic devices*
- *amount of time taken during breaks.*

Whatever method you use to collate these, make sure they are not open to any misinterpretation. Having clear ground rules will help your students feel comfortable and able to participate.

If your students attend sessions taken by other teachers, it is a good idea to discuss with them what your group has agreed, to ensure consistency. You might also take your students for other subjects and therefore have a core list of ground rules for all sessions, with some specific ones for each particular subject.

Ways to establish ground rules

A combination of both you and your students working together by a process of discussion and negotiation can be used. This enables your students to recognise what is and is not acceptable, giving them a sense of ownership and responsibility. It also enables students to begin working together as a group and encourages aspects such as listening, compromise and respect for others. Alternatively, your students could write down the rules individually, then discuss in pairs and join into fours to create a poster or a list on flipchart paper. One or two students could present this to the full group and agreement can then take place. Depending upon the age of your students, you could use the term *group contract* instead of ground rules. Ideally, the ground rules should be on display each time your group meets, and/or a typed version could be given to each student, or uploaded to a VLE if applicable.

Ways to maintain ground rules

Keeping the ground rules visible throughout the sessions will act as a reminder of what is not acceptable, and enable them to be amended or added to as necessary. Any students who have commenced the programme late will be able to see them. Always refer to the rules at the beginning of the session and when a rule is broken. For example, if a student is late, they must be reminded that it is a requirement that all lessons start promptly, otherwise they might not make the effort to arrive on time for subsequent sessions. If other students see that you don't say or do anything, they will feel the ground rules have no value. You could also refer to the ground rules when they are not broken as positive reinforcement of good behaviour.

If a student breaks a ground rule, you may find their peers reprimand them before you need to. However, you should always ask them to apologise to the others. You might like to ask your group to decide upon penalties or consequences for when a ground rule is broken. This could be a token penalty: for example, donating 50 pence to a group fund. Your students can then decide what to do with the fund at the end of the programme. It could be more serious: for example, writing their name on a wall chart and allocating a point every time a rule is broken. Three points could lead to disciplinary action or removal from the session. Ultimately, you will need to find your own strategy for dealing with students who break the ground rules, depending upon the age and maturity of the group. At the end of your session you could thank your students for following the ground rules; this will act as a reminder of their existence.

If you can lead by example, you will help create a culture of mutual compliance which should enable effective teaching and learning to take place.

Teaching and learning approaches

These will depend upon the subject you are teaching, the context and environment you are teaching in and the length of each session. However, you should choose approaches which will engage, stimulate and motivate your students. It's not about what you will teach, but what they will learn. Everything you do with your students should have a purpose, i.e. to enable learning to take place.

Formal teaching approaches include lectures, demonstrations and presentations which are usually teacher-centred, known as *pedagogy*. Informal approaches could include discussions, group work and practical activities and are usually student-centred, known as *andragogy*. Wherever possible it's best to use a mixture of the two and vary the approaches you use. This will ensure all learning styles are met and that all students are included and can participate.

Example

Zak teaches history in a college by lecturing to groups of students. He feels that although he uses a computerised presentation and handouts, his students are not actively participating in any way. He decides to make his session more practical by introducing group discussions and role plays of historical events. Several students approach him after the session to say how much they enjoyed it and how it enabled them to put theory into practice. He now uses this approach each time to mix knowledge and skills. He has set up the college's VLE to encourage interaction outside of the sessions, and to upload video and audio clips for students to access. He also finishes each session with a quiz to test knowledge gained.

Knowles et al. (2005) is the theorist who brought the concept of pedagogy and andragogy to the fore. The pedagogical approach places the responsibility for making decisions about the learning process upon the teacher, who may decide to teach the same material in the same order, at the same time to all students. This doesn't allow any flexibility for a student who may miss a session, or is learning more slowly or quickly than others.

The andragogical approach places the emphasis on the student to take responsibility for the learning process; they can then ensure they are learning in a way that suits them. This approach also allows the teacher to adapt their teaching materials to suit each student's progress and development. If your sessions are mainly pedagogical, try to include your students by asking individual questions to check their knowledge or by holding discussions. Your subject should never bore your students; you need to inspire them to maintain their motivation and interest. To help your confidence, imagine you are an actor playing a role. If you are nervous, stand tall, breathe deeply and pause for a second or two; it might seem a long time to you; however, it isn't. Focus your thoughts, relax and enjoy what you are doing. A tip if nerves do take over is to place your tongue on the roof of your mouth for a few seconds, no one will notice and you should feel better.

EDIP

EDIP is an acronym for **E**xplain, **D**emonstrate, **I**mitate and **P**ractice. Allen's (1919) four-step training method was originally devised for training shipyard workers in the United States. It is now widely used by the British and American forces and is a useful method when teaching a practical subject.

Explain clearly to your students in words they can understand all the main points of the task you are about to demonstrate, and why. Keep the points brief and simple.

Demonstrate the task slowly so that your students can see exactly what you have just explained. Make sure everyone can see what you are doing.

Imitate. Demonstrate the task again and this time ask your students to mirror and copy what you have just done. Watch them and reiterate the main points as they do it.

Practice. Ask your students to carry out the task on their own. Correct any errors and answer any questions they might have.

Delivering a session

When commencing a session, if you are unsure what to say to gather your students' attention, start with *Welcome to the session, today we will . . .* in a louder than normal but assertive voice. To settle your students and focus their attention towards learning, you could use a starter activity. This could be a quiz to test knowledge gained so far, a discussion to open up thinking about the current topic, or an energiser activity focusing upon the session topic. You can then state your aim and the objectives from your session plan. Always check if your students have any prior knowledge and/or experience by asking them; you can then draw upon this during the session. Never assume your students know or don't know something. As you teach, allow time for questioning, repeating and summarising important points. Incorporate the knowledge and experience of your students and if you can, give relevant anecdotes to bring the subject to life. Try not to use the word *obvious*, as things are only obvious to you. Show interest, passion and enthusiasm for your subject and encourage your students to take pride in their work. Use tone and inflection to emphasise key points and don't be afraid of silent pauses; they will give you time to refocus and your students time to consider what you have said. If you make a mistake, don't draw attention to it, but continue professionally; your students probably won't know any different. If you feel you are overrunning, don't be afraid to carry something over to the next session, or give it as homework. If you finish earlier than planned, make sure you have some extra activities you could use: for example, worksheets or a quiz. If particular students finish earlier than others, you could give them an extension activity to stretch and challenge their learning further.

If you are delivering a sequence of sessions, always recap the previous session before commencing the current session. While teaching, notice the reactions of your students; you might need to change your pace of delivery or introduce something practical to energise them. If you are demonstrating something in front of your students, always check if they are left- or right-handed as this could change the way they see things. When they look at you, your right hand will be on their left. If you are demonstrating one-to-one, try to stand next to your student rather than facing them. It's helpful to show a completed item if you are demonstrating how to make something: for example, a pipe weld or an iced cake. Make sure your session includes activities which cover all learning styles, i.e. visual, aural, read/write and kinaesthetic.

When you are planning break times, make sure you inform your students when these will be and for how long, otherwise they may be thinking about when they can get refreshments which will distract them from learning. If there is a break, when your students return, ask if they have any questions. Sometimes they will have been thinking about what they learnt before the break, and would like an opportunity to clarify aspects or ask questions. If possible, walk around the room regularly to ensure your students are not using electronic devices to communicate with their friends. If your students are using ICT equipment as part of the session (or laptops to make notes rather than using pen and paper), make sure you agree the boundaries of what sites can or cannot be accessed, and whether they can use social networking or e-mail.

If you find you have spare time towards the end of your session, there are a few things you can do. For example, ask each student in turn the *one thing* they have learnt during the session that has been most significant for them, with the reason why. This is good if you have a small group; however, if you have a large group you could approach it differently. Depending upon how much time you have, you could use the *one word* approach to gaining feedback from your students.

Example

Ellie had five minutes to spare at the end of her session. She decided to ask each of her 12 students to give her one word that summarised the session. If the word was negative she would ask the student to expand. Words included 'great', 'brilliant', 'fun' and 'boring'. She asked the student who had said 'boring' to explain why. He said he preferred to work on his own rather than get involved with group activities.

If Ellie had more time, she could have asked each student to expand on the positive as well as the negative points. Alternatively, she could ask for two, three or four word feedback. This makes students think a bit more about what they will say, and by limiting the words it keeps them focused.

Keeping some spare activities handy in case you have time can be a useful way to finish your session. You could create a worksheet, a crossword or a few multi-choice questions to use when necessary. For example, you could hold a quiz by placing your students in groups and letting them confer on the answers. If so, quickly think of a few questions regarding the topic your students have just learnt. A point could be allocated to the winning team and this method could be used more regularly as a fun way of finishing the session. It is also a good way to informally assess learning has taken place.

You should never let your students leave early as this could show you are disorganised, and they might come to expect it every time they are with you.

When you end your session, summarise the content, relate it to your aim and the objectives and explain what will be covered in the next session (if applicable). Plan time at the end for student questions and clearing up; you don't want to be rushed. If you are setting any homework, be clear about your requirements and hand in dates. Qualifications on the QCF require students to study in their own time, known as *non-contact time*. You will need to plan various activities for students to carry out as homework, i.e. reading, research, assignment, etc. Always follow up or check on their progress. If you are unsure what to say to formally end your session, simply say *Thank you*. If you are due to see your students again for another session, you could say *Thank you, I look forward to seeing you all again on. . .*

If you are teaching a session with a colleague, you will need to plan in advance which aspects will be covered by whom, and who will deal with any questions or behaviour issues. You will also need to plan who will introduce and close the session. Team teaching takes practice as personalities and teaching styles may differ. However, it is useful where a complex subject is being taught as different techniques of delivery can be utilised, and the experience and knowledge of the teachers drawn upon.

A mixture of different approaches within your sessions will ensure you meet all learning styles, engage your students, retain motivation and ensure learning is successful. Never be afraid to try something new and always evaluate how it went afterwards.

Table 5.1 opposite contains examples of teaching and learning approaches which you might like to try with your students. If you would like more information regarding these approaches, they are explained in detail in *Planning and Enabling Learning in the Lifelong Learning Sector* (2010) by Ann Gravells and Susan Simpson.

Extension Activity

Make a list of at least six different teaching and learning approaches you could use for your subject to engage and motivate your students. Consider the advantages and limitations of each and which are best suited to group or individual learning. You might like to refer to Table 5.1 opposite for some ideas. Choose one approach and plan how it will cover all learning styles.

Communication, behaviour and respect

Communication is a means of passing on information from one person to another. It is also a manner of expression: for example, your body language, voice and the gestures you make. The first time you meet your students they will probably make a subconscious judgement about you, and you will probably make one about them. These judgements often turn out to be wrong; therefore it is important not to make any assumptions about your students.

Body language includes facial expressions, eye contact, gestures, posture, non-verbal signals and appearance. Your personality will show through when you are teaching and there are some aspects you might not be able to control, such as facial flushing, blinking or clearing your throat. However, some you should control, such as winking, giving a thumbs-up sign or laughing. You need to be aware not only of your own body language, but that of your students. You need to sense what they are not saying as well as what they are saying.

Communication is the key to encouraging student motivation and respect, managing behaviour and disruption, and becoming a successful teacher. It should always be appropriate and effective, and to the level of your students. If you need to write on a board or flipchart while speaking to your students, don't do both at the same time. If you face the board, they may not hear you speak and you might miss something happening in the room.

Table 5.1 Teaching and learning approaches

Approach	Description
Activities	Tasks carried out by a group or individual, relevant to the topic being taught
Assignments	A longer-term activity based around the qualification or topic, which provides evidence of learning – can be practical or theoretical
Blended learning	Using more than one method of teaching, usually including technology. For example, a teaching session can be supported with learning materials and resources available via the organisation's VLE, with e-support/assessment from teachers as required
Buzz groups	Short topics to be discussed in small groups
Case studies	Can be a hypothetical situation, a description of an actual event or an incomplete event, enabling students to write or discuss how they would deal with it
Coaching	A one-to-one or small group activity which involves the teacher guiding the student – this is then followed by an observation of the student's performance
Debates	Knowledgeable group members or guests present a case to the students, with subsequent arguments, questions and discussions
Demonstration	A practical way of showing how something works
Dictation	Reading notes out loud for students to write down
Discussion	Students talk about a topic or the teacher can introduce a topic for the group to discuss
Distance learning or open learning	Learning and assessment which takes place away from the organisation offering the programme/qualification
Drawing	Illustrations to show how something works
E-learning (also see online learning)	Electronic learning – learning which is supported or enhanced using ICT. Audio and video can be utilised as well
Essays	A formal piece of written text, produced by the student, for a specific topic
Experiential/discovery	Practical tasks enabling students to experience or discover new knowledge and skills by carrying out activities.
Extension activity	An extra task to stretch and challenge students' learning further
Flexible learning	Learning that can take place at a time and place to suit the student and/or using different learning approaches
Games	A fun way of learning in pairs or groups to enable problem-solving and decision-making to take place
Gapped handout	Blank spaces within a handout can be used for students to complete
Group work	Enables students to carry out a specific activity: for example, problem-solving
Handouts	Written information/drawings, etc., to promote and support learning. A gapped handout will have missing words for students to complete
Homework	Activities carried out between sessions: for example, further reading, answering questions and research
Icebreakers/energisers	A fun and lighthearted way of introducing students and topics, or refocusing after a break
Instruction	Formal method of teaching whereby the teacher tells or shows the student what to do to achieve a particular skill; the student then performs this
Interviews	Practical activity to enable students to demonstrate skills and knowledge of a particular topic: for example, applying for a job
Journal or diary	Students keep a record of their progress, their reflections and thoughts
Lecture	Traditional teacher-centred technique of delivering information
Mentoring	One-to-one guidance and support by someone other than the teacher, who is experienced in the subject
Micro-teaching	A session taught by the student, usually in front of their peer group
Mind maps/spidergrams	A visual way of organising information and making plans; students draw a circle with a key point and branch from this with subheadings to explore and develop points further

Models	Designing and making relevant objects Life models, for example, in art classes
Online learning (also see e-learning)	Learning that takes place in a VLE via a computer connected to an intranet or the internet Asynchronous learning does not need to be accessed at fixed times or in real time Synchronous learning takes place in an environment where the teacher and student are simultaneously present, perhaps at different locations, but communicating with each other in real time
Recognition of prior learning (RPL)	Taking into account a student's prior knowledge, skills and achievements; as a result they do not have to retake aspects of a qualification again
Peer learning/ feedback	Students gaining skills and/or knowledge from their peers
Practical work	A task that students can carry out while the teacher observes progress, usually follows a demonstration or presentation
Presentations	Similar to a lecture, with greater use of audio-visual aids and interaction with students
Projects	A longer-term activity enabling students to provide evidence of or consolidate their learning towards a topic
Questions	A key technique for checking understanding and stimulating thinking. Open questions begin with who, what, when, where, why and how
Quizzes	Fun activities to test knowledge, skills and/or attitudes by the use of crosswords, panel games, etc.
Reading	Students work from relevant texts/books/journals/internet sites, etc.
Reports	Students produce a document to inform, recommend and/or make suggestions based on a given topic
Research	An in-depth way of finding out answers or more information regarding a topic
Role plays	Acting out a hypothetical situation or revisiting a real situation
Seminars	A presentation of ideas, followed by questions and a discussion
Simulation	An imitation activity carried out when the real activity would be too dangerous
Surveys	Students ascertain information from others regarding a particular topic, analyse and present their findings
Teaching/ training/ tutoring	Educating students in a subject, furthering their knowledge, skills and/or attitudes
Team teaching or co-teaching	Facilitating a session with a colleague
Technology-based learning	Using relevant equipment and materials: for example, interactive whiteboards/ videos/CD-ROMs/DVDs/the internet, etc.
Tests	Written questions (open, closed, multiple choice, etc.) to assess knowledge Practical activities to assess skills
Tutorials	A one-to-one or group discussion between the teacher and the student/s, with an agreed purpose: for example, discussing progress so far
Undoing	Students can undo or take apart an object, to learn how it was put together. An example is taking a plug apart to see how it was wired
Visiting speakers	An expert in the subject area speaks to the group
Visits/field trips	Students visit a venue relevant to the programme or qualification
Word shower (also known as brain storming)	A list of suggestions or ideas regarding a particular theme, topic or problem which should be agreed in groups without judgements or criticisms The list can then be refined and used as a basis for other activities, usually written on flipchart paper or a board so all students can see and take part
Worksheets	Interactive handouts to check knowledge (can also be electronic) Words can be circled, phrases completed, lists sorted, etc.
Workshops	Practical or simulated activities in a realistic working environment (RWE)

To get through a session without any disruptions would be wonderful, but this very rarely happens. You might have a student who arrives late, an inquisitive student who always wants to know more, or just someone asking to leave the room to get a drink of water. Whatever the disruption may be, you need to handle this professionally to minimise any effect it may have on teaching and learning. Don't just ignore the behaviour, address it immediately. However, with experience you will realise that some things can be ignored providing this does not affect the safety of your students.

Example

Philip was giving a presentation to a group of 15 students during an afternoon session. Three students in the group began talking among themselves about what they did at the weekend. Rather than reprimand them, Philip decided to stop speaking altogether and use eye contact with them. They soon realised he was no longer speaking but looking at them. Because he was silent, they stopped talking and paid attention again.

Usually, disruptions or changes in behaviour occur because a student doesn't follow the ground rules; for example, their mobile phone rings or they do something other than that which you have asked them to do. If this is the case, politely ask them to stop, remind them of the ground rules and how they are also disrupting their peers' learning. Other occurrences happen because people are bored, they don't understand what you are saying, their attention span is different, or you are not challenging them enough. You could give an alternative activity to stretch and challenge learning, get them involved with other students or have a quick one-to-one chat to find out why they are behaving that way.

You may find it useful to maintain a record of the behaviour of your students during your sessions to help you prepare for future incidents. For example, do some students become disruptive after a certain time period has elapsed; when seated in particular combinations with others, when asked to carry out a theory task, or when practical activities are taking place? This information can be useful when planning future sessions: for example, the timing of breaks, the use of energiser activities or planning group work. Behaviour patterns could highlight the need for additional support as disruption could be a way of asking for help. You should lead by example and always be polite, show respect and say *please* and *thank you* to help encourage this behaviour in your students. You should also promote respect between students by encouraging trust, honesty, politeness and consideration.

Your students may not be attending voluntarily, or they may be there for social reasons rather than having an interest in achieving a qualification. They may therefore not be as keen as you would like them to be and you will need to keep them continuously interested and motivated.

You can help maintain motivation and good behaviour by including all students during discussions and activities, keeping your sessions active wherever possible and teaching your subject in an interesting and challenging way. Ultimately, you need to find your own way of dealing with situations based upon your experiences. Don't show favouritism, lose your temper, make threats or touch students inappropriately. Try to have a positive approach, praise performance and good behaviour and be consistent and fair to everyone. Most students respond positively to a well-organised programme taught by an enthusiastic teacher who has a genuine interest in them and the subject.

Successful communication includes:

- oral communication, i.e. the way you speak when explaining, describing, summarising, questioning and giving feedback – be aware of your voice projection, tone and accent and when to use pauses to gain attention or allow thinking time

- written communication, i.e. presentations, handouts, worksheets, written feedback and progress reports – always check your spelling, grammar, punctuation and sentence construction

- non-verbal communication, i.e. the way you act, your body language, appearance, facial expressions, eye contact, gestures, posture and non-verbal signals

- questioning, i.e. oral or written to include all students, preferably using open questions

- listening skills, i.e. eye contact, not interrupting, not being judgemental

- skills such as empathy and sympathy.

The language you use should reflect equality and inclusiveness, be relevant to the subject, not offend anyone in any way and be at the right level and pitch for your students. You may have to practise with your voice projection, but don't shout, just speak louder and a little slower than normal and ask if students can hear you. Don't expect your students to remember everything first time; they don't know what you know. You should repeat or rephrase key points regularly. You might even get frustrated if asked questions regarding points you have already explained. Try not to say things like *I just told you that* or *Can't you remember what I just said?* Repeating key points will help your students remember them. Don't embarrass a student in front of their peer group; they may feel they can't ask you anything again. Learning occurs best in an active, not a passive, environment where communication is a two-way process. Always watch for signals from your students to check they are learning.

Example

Olga was explaining a complex topic and noticed one of her students, Josh, was making a strange expression, furrowing his brow as if he didn't understand. As Olga regularly uses eye contact with her students, she quickly spotted this and asked Josh if he would like her to explain the topic again. She rephrased what she had just explained and could see from his smiling and nodding face that he now understood. To double-check his learning, she asked an open question which required an answer other than Yes or No.

Dale (1969) devised the *cone of learning and experience* to express how people remember what they read, hear, see and do. Using activities from the top of the cone (passive) through to the bottom of the cone (active) will enable your students to realistically experience your subject. They should then remember more because they have *said and done* what they have *read and heard*, i.e. they have put theory into practice. The bands within the cone are not rigid but flexible, and the cone has been adapted and revised over the years.

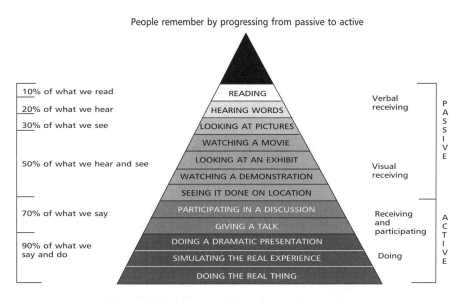

Figure 5.1 Dale's cone of learning and experience

Try to minimise any barriers to communication: for example, background noise, seating positions or the way you explain a topic. If a student asks a question, repeat this when you answer it so that everyone can hear what was asked. The same applies if a student answers a question as not everyone may hear this. Encourage your students to ask you questions, no matter how silly they think they are; probably another student is thinking the same but daren't ask. If you are asked something you don't know the answer to, say you will find out later and then make sure you do.

Effective listening takes place only when the person who receives the information interprets and understands it the way the deliverer intended. It can be easy to say something and think you said it in a way that your students will understand, only to find them asking you to say it again or to rephrase it.

To help your students hear you effectively, you should:

- speak clearly and slightly more loudly and slowly than normal
- not complicate your speech by including too much too soon or using too much jargon or too many acronyms
- not lose the point of what you are trying to put across
- remain focused
- ask open questions regularly to check your students are listening and understanding.

Activity

Read the following list of words once, cover them up and then write down the words you remember.

cat	*deck*	*table*	*snow*	*storm*
sky	*plant*	*book*	*smile*	*sky*
lulu	*lala*	*sky*	*plant*	*music*
tree	*bottle*	*money*	*cat*	*plant*

Among your words are probably cat, plant, sky, lulu and lala. This is because they occur at the beginning, the end, are unusual or repeated words. Use this approach with important points when teaching, i.e. by doing something different and repeating points. Ensuring you state your aim clearly at the beginning of your session; recapping regularly and summarising at the end will help learning take place. However, don't introduce anything new in your summary as this may confuse your students.

Extension Activity

Research different communication theories such as Eric Berne's (1964) Transactional Analysis and Belbin's (1993) Team Roles. How do these theories impact upon the role of the teacher when communicating with students?

Working with groups and individuals

Whether you work with groups or just individuals will influence the teaching and learning approaches you choose to take. You might be teaching a broad spectrum of ages from 14 upwards, either by age group, for example, 14–16 year olds, 16–19 year olds, or a mixture of younger and older students. Never assume or underestimate your students' knowledge or experience and try to draw on this during your sessions.

Working with an individual on a one-to-one basis may sound like the ideal method, but if your student is not committed to their learning, you will need to motivate them and of course keep your sessions interesting and stimulating.

When teaching groups of students, appreciate that they are a collection of individuals, and that each may behave differently in a group situation from when they are with other individuals. Group dynamics can change; for example, when new students commence, when the venue alters or if there are personality clashes. You will need to make new students welcome, perhaps buddying them with another student, or challenging behaviour and changing seating positions if there is disruption.

When facilitating group activities, make sure you give very clear instructions and a time limit. If the activity is to be carried out in small groups, knowledge of your students will help you decide if they have the maturity to group themselves or whether you need to group them. Consider which students will work together in case students with strong personalities dominate and change the group dynamics. Equally, make sure quiet students don't get left out and are able to participate. You might like to decide who will work with whom, or decide by their learning styles, levels of ability/experience, random names, or paired activities. Don't be afraid of trying something different; for example, giving your students responsibility for part of a session. Always remain in control and consider what you will be doing while they are working: for example, going around each group, listening, giving advice and encouragement, and reminding them of the time left.

When working with groups, you might like to consider Tuckman's (1965 and 1975) group formation theory of forming, storming, norming, performing and adjourning.

Forming This is the *getting to know you* and *what shall we do?* stage. Individuals may be anxious and need to know the boundaries and code of conduct within which to work.

Storming This is the *it can't be done* stage. It's where conflict can arise, rebellion against the leader can happen and disagreements may take place.

Norming This is the *it can be done* stage. This is where group cohesion takes place and the norms are established. Mutual support is offered, views are exchanged and the group co-operates.

Performing This is the *we are doing it* stage. Individuals feel safe enough to express opinions and there is energy and enthusiasm towards completing the task.

Adjourning This is the *we will do it again* stage. The task is complete and the group separates. Members often leave the group with the desire to meet again or keep in touch.

Extension Activity

Create an activity that you could use with a group of students for your specialist subject. Ensure you have a clear aim and a time limit. How large will each group be, why and how will you group them? Carry out the activity and see how far your students progress through Tuckman's stages.

Safeguarding and Every Child Matters

These are important aspects which form part of your responsibility as a teacher. You have a duty of care to ensure your students are able to learn and achieve in a safe environment.

Safeguarding

Safeguarding is a term used to refer to the duties and responsibilities that those providing a health, social or education service have to carry out/perform to protect individuals and vulnerable people from harm. Following the publication of the Safeguarding Vulnerable Groups Act in 2006, a vetting and barring scheme was established in autumn 2008. This Act created an Independent Barring Board to take all discretionary decisions on whether individuals should be barred from working with children and/or vulnerable adults. In 2006, the Department for Education and Skills (DfES) produced a document called *Safeguarding Children and Safer Recruitment in Education*. This guidance was aimed at local authorities, schools and further education colleges in England who are responsible for promoting the welfare of children and young people, up to the age of 18. Following this, the document *Safer Practice, Safer Learning* (NIACE, 2007) was produced to provide guidance in relation to adults in further education.

The Department of Health (DoH) (2000) document *No Secrets* specifies a definition of vulnerable adults.

> *A vulnerable adult is defined as a person 'who is or may be in need of community care services by reason of mental or other disability, age or illness; and who is or may be unable to take care of him or herself, or unable to protect him or herself against significant harm or exploitation'*

(Department of Health, 2000)

Safer Practice, Safer Learning (NIACE, 2007) recommends that safeguarding duties extend to whole-organisation policies, values and ethos, and include all staff and students. It is everyone's duty to promote the concepts of the safe student.

Every Child Matters

The Children Act 2004 provided the legal underpinning for the Every Child Matters: Change for Children programme. The term *student*, *adult* or *citizen* is often used when teaching post-16 students instead of *child*. Well-being is the term used in the Act to define the five Every Child Matters outcomes. Your organisation might expect you to take these into account when you are in contact with your students. These are:

- be healthy
- stay safe
- enjoy and achieve
- make a positive contribution
- achieve economic well-being.

> *A curriculum underpinned by Every Child Matters requires passionate and committed teaching that offers opportunities for open ended investigation, creativity, experimentation, teamwork and performance. It should also involve real experiences and activities.*
>
> (QCA, 2008, page 2)

Ways to embed the outcomes of Every Child Matters include:

- being healthy – access to drinking water and healthy food; opportunities to keep active
- staying safe – maintaining a safe environment; health and safety training
- enjoying and achieving – opportunities for all students to enjoy and contribute during sessions; recognising transferable skills; achieving a relevant qualification
- making a positive contribution – group activities, role play and teamwork; citizenship, voluntary work and work experience
- achieving economic well-being – business and enterprise activities; inviting visiting speakers from various professions, becoming independent and autonomous, gaining employment.

Extension Activity

How can you ensure the environment you teach in, and the people your students come into contact with, are deemed safe? Find out what the policies are at your organisation for Safeguarding, and Every Child Matters.

Summary

In this chapter you have learnt about:

● induction, icebreakers and ground rules

● teaching and learning approaches

● communication, behaviour and respect

● working with groups and individuals

● Safeguarding and Every Child Matters.

Cross-referencing grid

This chapter contributes towards the following: scope (S), knowledge (K) and practice (P) aspects of the Professional Teaching Standards (A–F domains) and the PTLLS units' assessment criteria. Full details of the learning outcomes and assessment criteria for each PTLLS unit can be found in the appendices.

Domain	Standards
A	ASI, AS2, AS3, AS6, AK2.I, AK2.2, AK3.I, AK5.I, AK6.I, AK6.2, API.I, AP2.I, AP2.2, AP6.I, AP6.2
B	BSI, BS2, BS3, BS5, BKI.I, BKI.2, BKI.3, BK2.I, BK2.2, BK2.3, BK2.4, BK2.5, BK2.7, BK3.I, BK3.2, BK3.3, BK3.4, BPI.I, BPI.2, BPI.3, BP2.I, BP2.2, BP2.3, BP2.4, BP2.5, BP3.I, BP3.2, BP3.3, BP3.4, BP3.5, BP5.I
C	CS2, CS3, CS4, CK2.I, CK3.I, CK3.2, CPI.2, CP2.I, CP3.I, CP3.5, CP4.2
D	DSI, DKI.I, DKI.2, DK2.I, DPI.I, DPI.2
E	
F	FK3.I, FPI.I, FPI.2, FP3.I, FP4.I, FP4.2

PTLLS unit	Assessment criteria	
	Level 3	Level 4
Roles, responsibilities and relationships in lifelong learning	3.I, 3.2	3.I, 3.2
Understanding inclusive learning and teaching in lifelong learning	I.I, I.2 2.I 3.2	I.I, I.2 2.I 3.2
Using inclusive learning and teaching approaches in lifelong learning	I.2 2.I, 2.3	I.2 2.I, 2.4
Principles of assessment in lifelong learning		

Theory focus

References and further information

Allen, CR (1919) *The Instructor: the man and the job: a hand book for instructors of industrial and vocational subjects.* USA: J B Lippincott Company.

Appleyard, N and Appleyard, K (2010) *Communicating with Learners in the Life-long Learning Sector.* Exeter: Learning Matters.

Belbin, M (1993, 1996, 2010) *Team Roles At Work.* Oxford: Elsevier Science & Technology.

Berne, E (1964, 1973, 2010) *Games People Play – The psychology of human relationships.* London: Penguin Books.

Dale, E (1969) *Audio Visual Methods in Teaching.* Texas: Holt Rinehart and Winston.

Department for Education and Skills (DfES) (2006) *Safeguarding Children and Safer Recruitment in Education.* London: DfES.

Department of Health (DoH) (2000) *No Secrets.* London: The Stationery Office.

Department of Health (DoH) Home Office and Department for Education and Employment (DfEE) (1999) *Working Together to Safeguard Children.* London: The Stationery Office.

Gelb, MJ (1988) *Present Yourself.* New York: Jalman.

Gravells, A and Simpson, S (2010) *Planning and Enabling Learning in the Lifelong Learning Sector* (2nd edn). Exeter: Learning Matters.

Hill, C (2008) *Teaching with e-learning* (2nd edn) Exeter: Learning Matters.

Knowles, MS, Holton, EF and Swanson, RA (2005) *The Adult Learner: The definitive classic in adult education and human resource development.* Oxford: Butterworth-Heinemann.

National Institute of Adult and Continuing Education (2007) *Safer Practice, Safer Learning.* Ashford: NIACE.

QCA (2008) *Every Child Matters at the Heart of the Curriculum.* London: QCA.

Reece, I and Walker, S (2008) *Teaching, Training and Learning: A practical guide* (6th edn). Tyne and Wear: Business Education Publishers.

Wallace, S (2007) *Managing Behaviour in the Lifelong Learning Sector* (2nd edn). Exeter: Learning Matters.

Websites

Every Child Matters shortcut – http://tinyurl.com/6dnfz93

Icebreakers – http://adulted.about.com/od/icebreakerstp/toptenicebreakers.htm

QCF shortcut – http://tinyurl.com/447bgy2

Tuckman – www.infed.org/thinkers/tuckman.htm

Introduction

In this chapter you will learn about:

- planning for assessment
- assessment types
- assessment methods
- making decisions and giving feedback
- assessment records

There are activities and examples to help you reflect on the above which will assist your understanding of how to assess learning. At the end of each section is an extension activity to stretch and challenge your learning further.

At the end of the chapter is a cross-referencing grid showing how the chapter's contents contribute towards the professional teaching standards and PTLLS units.

Planning for assessment

Assessment is a way of finding out if learning has taken place. It enables you to ascertain if your student has gained the required skills, knowledge and/or attitudes needed at a given point towards their programme of learning. If you don't plan for and carry out any assessment with your students, you will not know how well or what they have learnt.

Assessment can help your students by:

- diagnosing any areas of concern to enable support to be arranged
- encouraging discussions and questions
- ensuring they are on the right programme at the right level
- gaining feedback regarding what has been achieved so far, ascertaining areas for development and what is yet to be learnt and achieved
- maintaining motivation

- recognising what they have learnt

- seeing any mistakes they have made: for example, spelling, grammar and punctuation in a written task or errors during their performance.

Assessment is not another term for evaluation; assessment is *of the students* whereas evaluation is *of the programme*. Assessment is specific towards students' achievements and how they can improve. Evaluation includes feedback from your students and others to help you improve your own practice and the overall student experience.

Assessments are usually:

- internally set – produced by you, or your organisation: for example, questions or assignments, which will also be marked by you

- externally set – usually by an awarding organisation: for example, an assignment or examination. These will either be marked by you, a colleague, or by the awarding organisation that produced them.

Activity

Look at the syllabus or qualification handbook for the subject you will be assessing. What does it state your students must achieve? These are probably expressed in terms such as 'assessment criteria'. Are any assessment activities and materials provided for you or do you have to devise your own? If none is available, find out what is required and begin to create them.

The assessment cycle

Depending upon the subject you are assessing, and whether it is academic (i.e. knowledge) or vocational (i.e. performance), you will usually follow the assessment cycle (see Figure 6.1 on page 112). The cycle will continue until all aspects of the qualification have hopefully been achieved by your student, or perhaps not if they decide to leave the programme.

The cycle will then begin again with an initial assessment regarding the next subject area or unit of the qualification. Throughout the cycle, standardisation of assessment practice between assessors should take place; this will help ensure the consistency and fairness of decisions, and that you all interpret the requirements in the same way. Internal verification/quality assurance will also take place as part of the quality-assurance process. See Chapter 7 for further information.

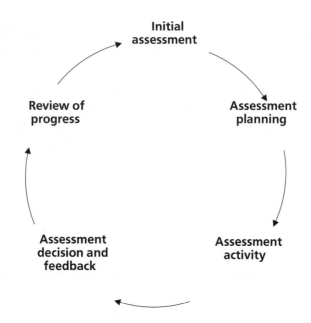

Figure 6.1 Assessment cycle

- Initial assessment – ascertaining if your student has any previous knowledge or experience of the subject to be assessed. Relevant initial assessment activities will also give you information regarding your students: for example, any specific assessment requirements they may have, their learning style, or any further training and support they may need.

- Assessment planning – agreeing suitable types and methods of assessment with each student, setting appropriate target dates, involving others as necessary: for example, colleagues or workplace supervisors, and following relevant organisational guidelines.

- Assessment activity – these relate to the methods used, i.e. assessor-led – for example, observation or questioning – or student-led: for example, completing assignments or gathering appropriate evidence of competence.

- Assessment decision and feedback – making a judgement of success or otherwise. Giving constructive feedback and agreeing any further action that may be necessary.

- Review of progress – the assessment plan can be reviewed and updated at any time until your student completes their programme or qualification. Reviewing progress with your students will give you an opportunity to discuss any other issues that may be relevant to their learning. Reviewing the assessment activities used will give you the opportunity to amend them if necessary.

Records should be maintained throughout all aspects of the assessment cycle.

Formal and informal assessments

Formal assessment activities will count towards your students' achievement of their qualification: for example, successful completion of an assignment, examination or test. The criteria for these will be stated in the syllabus or qualification handbook and will probably be known as assessment criteria and linked to the learning outcomes of the qualification. Formal assessments are usually completed with certain constraints such as a time limit or the amount of resources that can be used by students.

Informal assessment activities can take place at any time you are in contact with your students: for example, oral questions during a tutorial review, or a quiz or discussion at the end of a teaching session. Informal activities might not always count towards your students' achievement of their qualification, but will inform you how much learning is taking place.

Example

Cameron has taught a numeracy programme according to the syllabus, over three terms. At the end of each term, his students take an externally-set formal test provided by the awarding organisation. To plan for this, Cameron ensured he had delivered all the required content within the time, arranged for the classroom to be formally laid out with desks in rows, and forewarned his group of the date and time of the test. Prior to this he gave them an internally-devised test to check their progress. He had also been asking questions throughout the term to check knowledge. This informal assessment ensured that his students were ready for formal assessment.

Assessment should be a regular process; it might not always be formalised, but you should be observing what your students are doing, asking questions and reviewing their progress throughout their time with you.

Planning

Unless all your students are taking an examination or test on the same day at the same time, assessment should be planned for and carried out on an individual basis. Failing to plan how you are going to assess your students may result in your students failing the assessment activity. Assessment planning should be a two-way process between you and your students; you need to plan what you are going to do, and they need to know what is expected of them. If your students are all working towards the same assignment, you will still need to agree target dates for completion and discuss any specific requirements your students may have. If your students are to be assessed in their place of work, you will need to agree individual assessment activities and target dates. When planning for assessment, consider: *who, what, when, where, why* and *how*, to ensure both you and your student are aware of all the requirements.

You might need to complete an assessment plan or action plan with your students to formally document what they are aiming to achieve. This record is like a written contract between you and your student towards the achievement of their qualification. However, it can be reviewed, amended and updated at any time.

When planning for assessment, you need to ensure what you use will be valid and reliable, and that you are being fair and ethical.

- Valid – the assessment is appropriate to the subject/qualification and assesses only what it set out to.

- Reliable – if the assessment is carried out again with similar students, similar results will be achieved.

- Fair – the assessment is appropriate to all students at the required level, is inclusive, i.e. available to all, and differentiates for any particular needs.

- Ethical – the assessment takes into account confidentiality, integrity, safety and security.

These aspects must always be considered carefully, to ensure you are assessing only what is necessary and relevant, at a level to suit your students, and to ensure there is no favouritism. You also need to consider the environment in which you are assessing, i.e. that it is suitable, accessible and does not create any unnecessary barriers. Any resources you use should be relevant and effective. If you have students with any particular requirements, you need to consider how you can help meet their needs. Always check with your organisation what you can do as you may need formal approval to make any changes.

Example

If you have a dyslexic student, it may be appropriate to ask questions rather than give a written test, or have someone to scribe their responses. For a partially-sighted student you could give papers in a larger font or use a magnified reading lamp. For a deaf student, you could give a written test instead of an oral test. For a student with Asperger's syndrome, you could use illustrations to support text. For some students who might struggle with spelling and grammar, the use of a computer could help. An adapted keyboard or a pen grip could help a student with arthritis.

Some examples of meeting your students' needs include:
- adapting or providing resources and equipment
- adapting the environment
- allowing extra time

- arranging to use another language (e.g. Bilingual Welsh, British Sign Language)
- changing the date and/or time
- liaising with others who could offer advice or technical support
- maintaining constant contact and support: for example, via e-mail
- providing specialist support staff
- providing the assessment information in an alternative format
- using a different location which is more accessible
- using different assessment types and methods to suit learning styles
- using ICT and new and emerging technologies
- using larger print, Braille, or other alternative support mechanisms.

Always check with your awarding organisation to ensure you are following their regulations and requirements before making any changes. You may need to communicate with others who have an interest in your students' progress: for example, their employer, or others who also teach or assess your students.

Assessment planning should be inclusive to all, and always be specific, measurable, achievable, realistic and time-bound (SMART).

- **S**pecific – the activity relates only to the qualification and assessment criteria being assessed and is clearly stated.
- **M**easurable – the activity can be measured against the qualification and assessment criteria, allowing any gaps to be identified.
- **A**chievable – the activity can be achieved at the right level.
- **R**ealistic – the activity is relevant and will give consistent results.
- **T**ime bound – target dates and times are agreed.

You will need to take into account the possible contribution of any other people involved in the assessment process: for example, colleagues, managers, supervisors or witnesses. You should always inform your students when they can expect to receive any feedback or formal recognition of their achievements.

Extension Activity

Create an assessment plan or action plan for an individual student, which leads to a logical progression of achievement over a period of time. Ensure it is SMART and that the chosen assessment criteria can be achieved at the right level.

Assessment types

Assessment types include initial (at the beginning), formative (ongoing) and summative (at the end). Depending upon the subject you are assessing and the relevant awarding organisation's requirements, you might carry out various types of assessment with your students which could be on a formal or informal basis.

Initial assessment

This should take place prior to or when your students commence a particular programme or subject; see Chapter 3 for further information regarding initial diagnostic assessment. A quick question during your session, *Has anyone done this before?*, will soon give you some idea of what your students already know. Relevant initial assessment activities will also give you information regarding your students: for example, any specific assessment requirements or needs they may have, their learning style, or any further training and support they may need.

Formative assessment

Formative assessment should take place continually throughout your students' time with you and allow for development to take place. Simply asking questions and observing actions can help you give ongoing feedback to enable your students to develop further, before a summative or final assessment takes place.

Assessing your students on a formative basis will enable you to see if they are ready prior to a summative assessment. You could use activities, quizzes and short tasks for them to carry out which would make the assessment process more interesting and highlight any areas which need further development. If you are assessing a programme where the activities are provided for you, for example, examinations or tests, there is often a tendency to teach purely what is required for them to achieve a pass. Teaching to pass tests or examinations does not maximise a student's ability and potential and they may forget everything afterwards.

Summative assessments

Summative assessments usually occur at the end of a programme, topic, unit or full qualification. They can often be quite stressful to students and sometimes lead to a fail result even though the student is quite capable under other circumstances. However you assess your students, you must always make sure you are assessing only what needs to be assessed, i.e. the qualification requirements.

Assessment methods

The methods you use will depend upon whether you are assessing knowledge, skills or attitudes. Whether the awarding organisation states which methods you must use, or whether you choose your own, you need to treat each student as an individual, take into account equality and diversity and any particular student requirements.

Formal and informal assessment

Assessment methods are different from assessment types. A method is how the assessment type will be used and will be classed as formal or informal.

All assessment methods should be suited to the level and ability of your students. A level 1 student might struggle to maintain a journal; a level 2 student may not be mature enough to accept peer feedback; a level 3 student may feel a puzzle is too easy, and so on.

Table 6.1 Formal and informal assessment

Formal assessment methods include:	Informal assessment methods include:
● assignments	● discussions
● case studies	● gapped handouts
● essays	● journals/diaries
● examinations	● peer assessment
● multiple-choice questions	● puzzles and crosswords
● observations	● self assessment
● professional discussions	● questions – oral and written
● projects	● quizzes
● tests	● role plays
● witness testimonies	● worksheets

Questioning techniques

Questions are often the best way to assess knowledge. If you are asking questions verbally of a group of students, ensure you include all students. Don't just let the keen students answer first as this gives the ones who don't know the answers the chance to stay quiet. Ask a question, pause for a second and then state the name of a student who can answer. This way, all students are thinking about the answer as soon as you have posed the question, and are ready to speak if their name is asked. This is sometimes referred to as 'pose, pause, pounce' (PPP). To ensure you include everyone throughout your session, you could have a list of their names handy and tick each one after you have asked them a question. If a student doesn't know the answer, ask them to guess. That way they have to think and can't opt out. If they guess wrongly, state it was a good attempt and then ask another student. When asking questions, use only one question in a sentence, as more than one may confuse your students. Try not to ask *Does anyone have any questions?*, as often only those who are keen or confident will ask, and this doesn't tell you what your students have learnt. Try not to use questions such as *Does that make sense?* or *Do you understand?*, as your students will often say *Yes* as they feel that's what you expect to hear.

Try to use open questions which require an answer to demonstrate knowledge and understanding. For example, *How many days are there in September?* This ensures your student has to think about their answer. Using a closed question such as *Are there 30 days in September?* would give only a yes/no answer which doesn't show you if your student has the required knowledge. Open questions usually begin with *who, what, when, where, why* and *how*.

If you are having a conversation with your student, you can ask probing questions to ascertain more information. These can begin with: *Why was that?* You can prompt your student to say more by asking *What about. . .?* You can also clarify what your student is saying by asking *Can you go over that again?*

If you have to write your own questions for students, think how you will do this, i.e. short questions, essay-style questions, open, closed or multiple choice. If you are giving grades, e.g. A, B, C, or pass/merit/distinction, you need clear grading criteria to follow to make sure your decisions are objective, otherwise your students may challenge your decisions.

Example

Summative assessment is always:

A   before the programme commences
B   at the beginning of the programme
C   in the middle of the programme
D   at the end of the programme

You will see that all the answers contain a similar amount and type of words. None of the answers contains a clue from the question. A, B and C are the distracters and D is the correct answer (the key).

Multiple-choice questions should have a clear question and three or four possible answers. The question is known as the stem, the answer is called the key and the wrong answers are called distracters. Answers should always be similar in length and complexity. Answers should not be confusing, and there should be only one definite key.

If you are using the same questions for different students at different times, be careful as they may pass the answers to each other. You may need to rephrase some questions if your students are struggling with an answer, as poor answers are often the result of poor questions. For essay and short-answer tests you should create sample answers to have something to compare with. Be careful with the use of jargon – just because you understand doesn't mean your students will.

You need to be aware of plagiarism, particularly now that so much information is available via the internet. Students should take responsibility for referencing any sources of all work submitted, and may be required to sign an authenticity statement. If you suspect plagiarism, you could type a few of their words into an internet search engine or specialist program and see what appears. You would then have to challenge your student as to whether it was intentional or not, and follow your organisation's plagiarism procedure.

Observation

Observation is a good way to assess skills and attitudes. Observing your students enables you to see just how well they are doing. Let your student make a mistake (if it is safe) rather than interrupt them as they will learn from their mistakes. You can then ask them afterwards to see if they realised. You can also observe group work and presentations; this can encourage students to give peer feedback. You would need to make a decision as to the contribution of each student if their work was part of a group activity. Observations are useful in the workplace to assess your students' competence, skills and attitudes. You can always follow an observation with questions to check knowledge and understanding.

Peer and self-assessment

Peer assessment involves a student assessing another student's progress. Self-assessment involves a student assessing their own progress. Both methods encourage students to make decisions about what has been learnt so far, and to reflect on aspects for further development. Your students will need to fully understand the assessment criteria, and how to be fair and objective with their judgements. Throughout the process of peer and self-assessment, students can develop skills such as listening, observing and questioning.

Table 6.2 overleaf gives the advantages and limitations of each.

Table 6.2 Advantages and limitations of peer and self-assessment

Peer assessment advantages are that:	Peer assessment limitations include:
• they can reduce the amount of teacher assessment • they increase attention for activities such as peer presentations if feedback has to be given • students are more focused upon the assessment criteria • students may accept comments from peers more readily than those from the assessor • they promote student and peer interaction and involvement.	• all peers should be involved therefore planning needs to take place as to who will give feedback and to whom • appropriate conditions and environment are needed • assessor needs to confirm each student's progress and achievements as it might be different from their peers' judgement • everyone needs to understand the assessment criteria • students might be subjective and friendly rather than objective with their decisions • needs to be carefully managed to ensure no personality conflicts or unjustified comments • should be supported with other assessment methods • some peers may be anxious, nervous or lack confidence to give feedback.
Self-assessment advantages are that:	**Self-assessment limitations include:**
• it encourages students to check their own progress • it encourages reflection • mistakes can be seen as opportunities • it promotes student involvement and personal responsibility	• assessor needs to discuss and confirm progress and achievement • difficult to be objective when making a decision • students may feel they have achieved more than they actually have • students must fully understand the assessment criteria • students need to be specific about what they have achieved and what they need to do to complete any gaps • some students may lack confidence in their ability to make decisions about their own progress

Activity

What activities could you use with your students to promote peer and/or self assessment? How would you manage the process so that everyone was being fair and objective?

Peer assessment can also be useful to develop and motivate students. However, this should be managed carefully, as you may have some students who do not get along and might use the opportunity to demoralise one another. You would need to give advice to your students as to how to give feedback effectively. If student feedback is given skilfully, other students may think more about what their peers have said than about what you have said. If you consider peer assessment has a valuable contribution to make to the assessment process, ensure you plan for it to enable your students to become accustomed and more proficient at giving it. The final decision as to the competence of your student will lie with you.

Examples of peer and self-assessment activities include students:

- assessing each other's work anonymously and giving written or verbal feedback
- completing checklists, templates or pro-formas
- giving grades and/or written or verbal feedback regarding own or peer presentations
- holding group discussions before collectively agreeing a grade and giving feedback, perhaps for a presentation
- suggesting improvements to their own or peers' work
- producing a written statement of how they could improve their own or peers' work

Extension Activity

Review and evaluate the assessment activities that you could use for your particular subject. Are they pitched at the right level and will they fully assess the criteria? What do you consider to be their strengths and limitations?

Table 6.3 on pages 122 and 123 lists some of the assessment methods you might wish to use. A more comprehensive list can be found in the book *Achieving your TAQA Assessor and Internal Quality Assurance Award* by Ann Gravells.

Table 6.3 Assessment methods

Method	Description	Strengths	Limitations
Assignments	Several activities or tasks to cover theory and practice	Can challenge your student's potential or consolidate learning A well-written project will help your student provide evidence of knowledge, skills and attitudes	Ensure all aspects of the syllabus have been taught beforehand Must be individually assessed and written feedback given
Discussions/debates	Students talk about a relevant subject which contributes to the assessment criteria	All students can participate Allows freedom of viewpoints, questions and discussions	Assessor needs to keep the group focused and set a time limit Some students may not get involved, others may take over
E-assessments/online assessments	Assessment using ICT	Can take place at a time to suit students Participation is widened Results can be instantly generated Less paperwork for the assessor	Students need to be computer literate Authenticity of students' work may need validating Technical support may be required
Essays	Formal pieces of written text	Useful for academic subjects Can check your students' language and literacy skills at specific levels	Marking can be time-consuming Plagiarism can be an issue Students need good writing skills
Examinations	Formal tests which should be carried out in certain conditions	Can be *open book*, or *open notes*, enabling students to have books and notes with them	Some students may be anxious Students may have been taught purely to pass expected questions, therefore they may forget everything afterwards
Journal/diaries	Students keep a record of their progress, their reflections and thoughts, and reference these to the assessment criteria	Develop self-assessment skills Relate theory to practice Help assess language and literacy skills Useful for higher-level programmes	Should be specific to the learning taking place and be analytical rather than descriptive Can be time-consuming to read
Observations	Watching students perform a skill	Enable skills to be seen in action Can assess several aspects of a qualification at the same time (holistic)	Timing must be arranged to suit your student, communication needs to take place with others (if in your student's working environment)
Peer assessments	Students giving feedback to each other	Promote student involvement Activities can often correct misunderstandings and consolidate learning without intervention by the assessor	There may be personality clashes resulting in subjective decisions Need careful management and training in how to give feedback
Portfolios of evidence	Formal records of evidence (manual or electronic) to meet the assessment criteria	Can be compiled over a period of time Student-centred, promotes autonomy	Authenticity and currency to be checked Tendency for students to produce too much Can be time-consuming to assess

Method	Description	Strengths	Limitations
Professional discussions	Conversations between the assessor and student based around the assessment criteria	Ideal way to assess aspects which are more difficult to observe, or to complete any identified gaps from other assessments	A record must be kept of the discussion Need careful planning
Puzzles, quizzes, word search, crosswords, etc.	Fun ways of assessing learning in an informal way	Useful backup activity if students finish an activity earlier than planned Good way to assess progress of lower-level students and retention of facts	Can seem trivial to mature students Does not assess your students' level of understanding or ability to apply their knowledge to situations
Questions – oral or written	A key technique for assessing understanding and stimulating thinking	Can challenge your students' potential Can test critical arguments or thinking and reasoning skills	Questions must be unambiguous If the same questions are used with other students, they could share the answers Expected responses need to be produced
RPL	Assessing what has previously been learnt to find a suitable starting point for further assessment	Ideal for students who have achieved aspects of the programme already No need for students to duplicate work, or be reassessed	Checking the authenticity and currency of the evidence provided is crucial Can be time-consuming for both your students to prove, and you to assess
Role plays	Students act out a hypothetical situation	Encourage participation Can lead to debates Link theory to practice	Can be time-consuming Clear role must be defined Not all students may want or be able to participate
Self-assessments	Students decide how they have met the criteria, or are progressing at a given time	Promote student involvement and personal autonomy Encourage students to check their own work before handing it in	Students may feel they are doing better than they actually are
Tests	Formal assessment situations	Cost-effective method as the same test can be used with large numbers of students Some test responses can be scanned into a computer for marking and analysis	Needs to be carried out in supervised and timed conditions Can be stressful to students Feedback may not be immediate Students taking a test before others may communicate the answers
Witness testimonies	Statements from a person who knows the student	The witness can confirm competence or achievements, providing they are familiar with the assessment criteria; for example a workplace supervisor	The assessor must confirm the suitability of the witness and check the authenticity of any statements
Worksheets and gapped handouts	Interactive handouts to check knowledge (manual or electronic) Blank spaces can be used for students to fill in the missing words	Informal assessment activity which can be carried out individually, in pairs or groups Useful for lower-level students and differentiation	Mature students may consider them inappropriate Too many worksheets can be boring, students might not be challenged enough

Making decisions and giving feedback

Making decisions

The decisions you make regarding your students' progress can affect them both personally and professionally. It's important to remain factual about what you have assessed and to be objective with your judgements. You should never compromise and pass a student just because you like them, feel they have worked hard or are under pressure to achieve targets.

When making a decision, check for VACSR:

- **V**alid – the work is relevant to the assessment criteria.

- **A**uthentic – the work has been produced solely by the student.

- **C**urrent – the work is still relevant at the time of assessment.

- **S**ufficient – the work covers all the assessment criteria.

- **R**eliable – the work is consistent across all students, over time and at the required level.

You will need to complete relevant records to prove that assessment took place. Usually, you will keep the original document and give your student a copy. This is because it is more difficult to forge a copy than an original document.

Reviewing progress

It is important to review your students' progress regularly, as this gives you the opportunity to discuss on a one-to-one basis how they are progressing, what they may need to improve and what they have achieved. Often, this is formally documented and signed by both parties so that records of the discussion are maintained.

Reviews are a good opportunity to carry out formative assessments in an informal way. They also give your student the chance to ask questions they might have been embarrassed about asking in a group situation.

Giving feedback

All students need to know how they are progressing, and what they have achieved. Feedback should help reassure, boost confidence, encourage and motivate. Feedback can be given formally, i.e. in writing, or informally, i.e. verbally, and should be given at a level which is appropriate for each student. Feedback can be direct, i.e. to an individual, or indirect, i.e. to a group. It should be more thorough than just a quick comment such as 'Well done' and should include specific facts which relate to progress, success or otherwise in order to help your students develop.

You could always ask your students first how they think they have done. For example, if you have just observed them perform a task and they made a mistake it gives them the opportunity to say so before you need to.

Activity

Think back to the last time you received feedback from someone for something you did. Was this feedback constructive? Did it leave you feeling motivated and good about what you had done? Or did it leave you feeling demotivated and not willing to continue?

If possible, feedback should be a two-way process, allowing a discussion to take place to clarify any points. If you are giving verbal feedback, be aware of your body language, facial expressions and tone of voice. Don't use confrontational words or phrases likely to cause offence such as racist or stereotypical remarks. Take into account any non-verbal signals from your students; you may need to adapt your feedback if you see they are becoming uncomfortable. If you are giving written or electronic feedback consider that how your student reads it may not be how you intended it.

Feedback should never just be an evaluative statement like *Well done*, or *That's great, you've passed*. This doesn't tell your student what was done well, or was great about it. Your student will be pleased to know they have passed; however, they won't have anything to build upon for the future.

Descriptive feedback lets you describe what your student has done, how they have achieved and what they can do to progress further. It enables you to provide opportunities for your student to make any adjustments or improvements to reach a particular standard.

Skinner (1968), a behaviour theorist, argued that students need to make regular active responses. These responses need immediate feedback with differential follow-ups depending upon whether or not they were correct. Without immediate feedback, especially when the response is wrong, your student will carry on making the same mistake thinking they are right. They will then have to unlearn their response. Time can be wasted by students unlearning their wrong responses instead of learning new behaviours.

Most people need encouragement, to be told when they are doing something well and why. When giving feedback it can really help your student to hear first what they have done well, followed by what they need to improve, and then end on a positive note to keep them motivated. This is known as the 'praise sandwich'. Often, the word *but* is used to link these points; replacing this with the word *however* is much easier for your student to accept.

Using your student's name makes the feedback more personal, and making the feedback specific enables your student to see what they need to do to improve. You will need to find out from your organisation how they require you to give feedback: for example, writing in the first, second or third person. You also need to know whether it should be given verbally and/or written; formally or informally; how much detail should be given; what forms must be completed; and what records must be maintained.

The advantages of giving constructive feedback are that it:

- creates opportunities for clarification and discussion
- emphasises progress rather than failure
- helps improve confidence and motivation
- identifies further learning opportunities or any action required.

You could ask for feedback from your students as to how they felt about the assessment process. This will help you improve your own skills or to pass on information to the Awarding Organisation if necessary.

Extension Activity

Research different feedback methods: for example, evaluative and descriptive; constructive and destructive; objective and subjective. Consider the strengths and limitations of each and decide which methods are best suited to your subject along with the reasons why.

Assessment records

Records must be maintained to satisfy your organisation's internal quality-assurance systems, and external regulators such as Ofsted, and the awarding organisation's requirements. Assessment records must show an audit trail of your students' progress from commencement to completion and are usually kept at your organisation for three years. If a student loses their work, without any assessment records you have nothing to show that you actually assessed it. If you are teaching a programme which does not lead to a formal qualification, i.e. non-accredited, you will still need to record student progress. This is known as recognising and recording progress and achievement (RARPA).

Records must be up to date, accurate, factual and legible whether they are stored manually or electronically. If you are saving to a computer, always ensure you have a backup copy in case any data are lost. You must always maintain confidentiality and follow relevant legislation such as the Data Protection Act (2003), which is mandatory for all organisations that hold or process personal data. The Freedom of Information Act (2000) gives your students the opportunity to request to see the information your organisation holds about them. Keeping full and accurate factual records is also necessary in case one of your students appeals against an assessment decision. If this happens, don't take it personally; they will be appealing against your decision, not you.

Table 6.4 Assessment records

The types of assessment records you might maintain include:	You might also use and need to maintain other records such as:
• achievement dates and grades, e.g. pass/refer • assessment plan and review records • assessment tracking sheet showing progression through a qualification for all students • diagnostic test results • feedback and action records • initial assessment records • learning styles results • observation checklists • performance and knowledge records • professional discussion records • progress reports • records of achievement • records of oral questions and responses	• action plans • appeals records • application forms • authentication statements • checklists • CPD records • copies of certificates • enrolment forms • observation reports • receipts for assignments • register or record of attendance • retention and achievement records • standardisation records • tutorial reviews • unit declarations • witness testimonies

Extension Activity

Make a list of all the assessment records you would use for your subject. What improvements could you make to simplify them, whilst maintaining a full audit trail of student achievement? What organisational or regulatory requirements must you follow regarding assessment records and why?

Summary

In this chapter you have learnt about:

- planning for assessment
- assessment types
- assessment methods
- making decisions and giving feedback
- assessment records.

Cross-referencing grid

This chapter contributes towards the following: scope (S), knowledge (K) and practice (P) aspects of the Professional Teaching Standards (A–F domains) and the PTLLS units' assessment criteria. Full details of the learning outcomes and assessment criteria for each PTLLS unit can be found in the appendices.

Domain	Standards
A	ASI, AS5, AS7, AK6.I, AK6.2, AK7.I, API.I, AP2.I, AP7.I
B	BS3, BS4, BK2.5, BK3.2, BK3.4, BK5.I, BP2.I, BP2.3, BP2.5, BP3.2, BP4.I
C	CS2, CS3, CK3.2, CP3.2
D	DS2, DKI.I, DK2.I, DK2.2, DP2.2
E	ESI, ES2, ES3, ES4, ES5, EKI.I, EKI.2, EKI.3, EK2.I, EK2.2, EK2.3, EK2.4, EK3.I, EK3.2, EK4.I, EK4.2, EK5.I, EK5.2, EK5.3, EPI.I, EPI.2, EPI.3, EP2.I, EP2.2, EP2.3, EP2.4, EP3.I, EP3.2, EP4.I, EP4.2, EP5.I, EP5.2, EP5.5
F	

PTLLS unit	Assessment criteria	
	Level 3	Level 4
Roles, responsibilities and relationships in lifelong learning		
Understanding inclusive learning and teaching in lifelong learning	2.3 3.3	2.3 3.3
Using inclusive learning and teaching approaches in lifelong learning	1.3 2.4	2.3 2.5
Principles of assessment in lifelong learning	1.1, 1.2, 1.3, 2.1, 2.2 3.1, 3.2	1.1, 1.2, 1.3, 2.1, 2.2 3.1, 3.2

Theory focus

References and further information

Gravells, A (2011) *Principles and Practice of Assessment in the Lifelong Learning Sector* (2nd edn). Exeter: Learning Matters.

Gravells, A (2012) *Achieving your TAQA Assessor and Internal Quality Assurer Award*. Exeter: Learning Matters.

Ofqual (2009) *Authenticity – A Guide for Teachers*. Coventry: Ofqual.

Skinner, BF (1968) *The Technology of Teaching*. New York: Appleton, Century and Crofts.

Tummons, T (2011) *Assessing Learning in the Lifelong Learning Sector*. Exeter: Learning Matters.

Websites

Assessment guidance booklets –
www.sflip.org.uk/assessment/assessmentguidance.aspx

Assessment methods in higher education –
www.brookes.ac.uk/services/ocsld/resources/methods.html

Assessment tools (literacy, numeracy, ESOL, dyslexia) –
www.excellencegateway.org.uk/toolslibrary

Chartered Institute for Educational Assessors – www.ciea.org.uk

Data Protection Act (2003) –
http://regulatorylaw.co.uk/Data_Protection_Act_2003.html

Dyslexia Association – www.dyslexia.uk.net

Freedom of Information Act (2000) –
www.opsi.gov.uk/Acts/acts2000/ukpga_20000036_en_1

Initial assessment –
www.excellencegateway.org.uk/page.aspx?o=nav-resources&node=8436

Learning styles – www.vark-learn.com

Ofsted – www.ofsted.gov.uk

Plagiarism – www.plagiarism.org and www.plagiarismadvice.org

RARPA – http://archive.niace.org.uk/projects/RARPA/Default.htm

7   QUALITY ASSURANCE AND EVALUATION

Introduction

In this chapter you will learn about:

- quality assurance
- evaluation
- self-reflection and learning journals
- Continuing Professional Development
- progression

There are activities and examples to help you reflect on the above which will assist your understanding of what quality assurance is and how to evaluate yourself and the programmes you have taught. At the end of each section is an extension activity to stretch and challenge your learning further.

At the end of the chapter is a cross-referencing grid showing how the chapter's contents contribute towards the professional teaching standards and PTLLS units.

Quality assurance

All programmes should follow a quality assurance system to ensure they are being delivered and assessed fairly, consistently and accurately. You might not be involved with all aspects of quality assurance at your organisation; however, they will impact upon your role, therefore you should familiarise yourself with the requirements. Quality assurance can be internal, i.e. issuing student surveys, updating policies and procedures and observing teaching sessions. It can also be external, i.e. inspectors, auditors and verifiers visiting to check compliance.

Information gained from aspects of quality assurance must lead to improvements for your students, yourself and your organisation.

Activity

Have a look at the example in Figure 7.1 below of a quality assurance cycle and describe how each aspect could impact upon your role as a teacher.

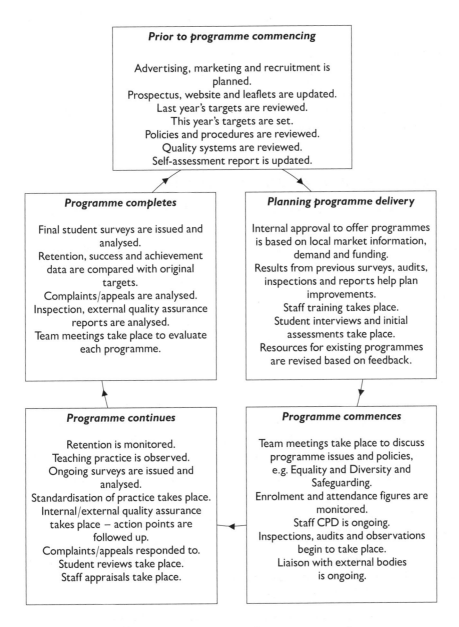

Prior to programme commencing

Advertising, marketing and recruitment is planned.
Prospectus, website and leaflets are updated.
Last year's targets are reviewed.
This year's targets are set.
Policies and procedures are reviewed.
Quality systems are reviewed.
Self-assessment report is updated.

Programme completes

Final student surveys are issued and analysed.
Retention, success and achievement data are compared with original targets.
Complaints/appeals are analysed.
Inspection, external quality assurance reports are analysed.
Team meetings take place to evaluate each programme.

Planning programme delivery

Internal approval to offer programmes is based on local market information, demand and funding.
Results from previous surveys, audits, inspections and reports help plan improvements.
Staff training takes place.
Student interviews and initial assessments take place.
Resources for existing programmes are revised based on feedback.

Programme continues

Retention is monitored.
Teaching practice is observed.
Ongoing surveys are issued and analysed.
Standardisation of practice takes place.
Internal/external quality assurance takes place – action points are followed up.
Complaints/appeals responded to.
Student reviews take place.
Staff appraisals take place.

Programme commences

Team meetings take place to discuss programme issues and policies, e.g. Equality and Diversity and Safeguarding.
Enrolment and attendance figures are monitored.
Staff CPD is ongoing.
Inspections, audits and observations begin to take place.
Liaison with external bodies is ongoing.

Figure 7.1 Example of a quality assurance cycle

Standardisation of practice

Standardisation enables consistency and fairness of teaching and assessment. If more than one person is teaching and/or assessing the same qualification, it is important that they all agree how to interpret the requirements, deliver the content and make assessment decisions. Attending a standardisation meeting is also an opportunity to develop and share good practice and be part of a team. It is best to meet prior to the programme commencement to discuss the qualification requirements, design the scheme of work, assessment activities and any resources. Once assessments have taken place, another meeting can be held to bring examples of assessment decisions to compare and discuss. Double or blind marking can take place, whereby another assessor marks the work (with or without seeing the original feedback and grade) to ensure consistency and fairness.

Internal verification and moderation

Internal verification (also known as internal quality assurance) should be carried out by another member of staff who is qualified and experienced in your subject area. They will validate a sample of your assessment decisions and give you feedback and advice. If a problem is found with a student's work, they will have the chance to correct it. Another form of quality assurance is internal moderation. With this method, if the internal moderator finds problems with a particular area sampled, all students' work for this area will need to be re-checked.

Observations

You will probably be observed at some time when you are teaching or assessing. This might be by your internal quality assurer, line manager, external verifier, inspector or mentor. You should be notified beforehand and it's important to have all your records available, i.e. scheme of work, session plans, assessment results, register, etc. Your observer may also talk to your students about their progress. You should receive feedback which will help you improve your future practice.

Extension Activity

If you are currently teaching, ask a colleague or your mentor to observe one of your sessions. Use the feedback as an opportunity to improve your practice. Then ask if you could observe one of their sessions.

If you are not currently teaching, ask your PTLLS teacher if they could put you in touch with someone who would be willing to let you observe them. Seeing how an experienced teacher delivers their subject should give you some useful ideas for when you do become a teacher. The checklist in Appendix 9 should prove helpful when you begin teaching.

Evaluation

Whichever type of programme you teach, short- or long-term, it is important to evaluate the teaching and learning process. This should be an ongoing procedure throughout all aspects of the teaching and learning cycle. It will help you realise how effective you were and what you could change or improve: for example, using different types of resources. It will also help you identify any problem areas, enabling you to do things differently next time. Using feedback from others, information and data is the best way to evaluate the programme you have taught. Never assume everything is going well just because you think it is.

Obtaining feedback

Feedback can come from surveys and questionnaires, reviews, appraisals and informal and formal discussions and meetings. Other information to help you evaluate your programme includes statistics such as retention, success and achievement rates which can affect the amount of funding received. All feedback should help evaluate whether teaching and learning have been successful (or not) as well as help you to improve your own practice and inform future planning.

If you have taught a one-day or short programme, you might give your students a questionnaire at the end. Always build in time to your session for this to take place, otherwise your students may take away the questionnaire and forget to return it. It could contain closed questions such as

Were the teaching and learning approaches suitable? Yes/No

or open questions such as

How did you find the teaching and learning approaches?

The latter is best as you should gain more information. When issuing questionnaires, decide whether you want the responses to be anonymous or not, as you might gain more feedback if students know they are unidentifiable.

You might decide to use a mixture of open and closed questions. Open questions always require a full response and give you *qualitative* data to work with; closed questions get only a yes or no answer and give you *quantitative* data. If you use a closed question, follow this up with an open question to enable you to obtain further information.

Example

1. **Did the programme fulfill your expectations? Yes/No**
   How did it achieve this?
2. **Were the teaching methods and resources appropriate? Yes/No**
   Why was this?
3. **Was the venue suitable? Yes/No**
   What did/didn't you like about it?
4. **Did you enjoy your learning experience? Yes/No**
   What did/didn't you like?
5. **Have you gained the skills and knowledge you expected to? Yes/No**

There are many ways of writing questions to gain different types of responses. A closed question could be followed by a response scale of 1–5 for students to circle

(1 being no or low, 5 being yes or high); for example:

Did the programme fulfill your expectations?   1   2   3   4   5

The tendency might be to choose number 3 as it is in the middle. Removing a number makes the response more definitive one way or the other; for example:

Did the programme fulfill your expectations?   1   2   3   4

Instead of numbers, you could use smiley faces for students to circle. For example:

Did the programme fulfill your expectations?   ☹   ☺   ☺

Having fewer options should help to gain a realistic response. Whatever you decide to ask, make sure you keep your questions simple: don't ask two questions in one sentence or use complicated jargon, allow space for written responses and thank your students for their contributions. Always analyse the responses and inform your students how their contributions have led to changes and improvements.

Talking to your students informally will help you realise how successful teaching and learning has been. This can be done during reviews, at break times or before or after your sessions. Your students are the best judges of whether they are getting what they feel they need. If given the opportunity, they may give you more feedback in an informal situation.

If you are teaching a longer programme, it is useful to obtain feedback part-way through, as well as at the end. This will enable you to make any necessary changes. Evaluation and feedback can contribute to your organisation's quality cycle by helping improve the service given to students.

Design a short questionnaire that you could use with your own students. Consider what information you would like to know and why, and then write your questions carefully. If you are currently teaching, compare your questionnaire with ones currently used in your organisation. Use the questionnaire with your students, collate the responses and write a short report as to what changes you would make as a result of the feedback gained. If possible, implement the changes.

Self-reflection and learning journals

When teaching, you are also learning about yourself. For example, how you react to different situations or students, how patient you are and what skills you may need to develop. You may also decide you need further training to improve your subject knowledge and/or literacy, language and numeracy skills. Self-reflection should take place after each session you teach, or any significant incident, to consider what went well and what could be improved. For example, you could ask yourself if you used eye contact with each student and addressed everyone by name at some point during the session. If your answer is *No* then next time ensure that you do. Another question to ask yourself is, *How do I know that learning has taken place?* If you can't answer this, you will need to make some changes to your teaching and assessment methods.

Reflection is often just your thoughts which can be positive or negative but can take into account any feedback you have received. It is useful to keep a learning journal to note anything important; you can then refer to this when planning your future development or preparing your teaching sessions. Reflection is about becoming more self-aware, which should give you increased confidence and improve the links between the theory and practice of teaching and learning.

A straightforward method of reflection is to have the experience, then describe it, analyse it and revise it (EDAR). This method should help you think about what has happened and then consider ways of changing and/or improving it. See Table 7.1 on page 136 for an example of a learning journal.

Experience → Describe → Analyse → Revise

EDAR

- *Experience* – a significant event or incident you would like to change or improve.
- *Describe* – aspects such as *who* was involved, *what* happened, *when* it happened and *where* it happened.
- *Analyse* – consider the experience deeper and ask yourself *how* it happened and *why* it happened.
- *Revise* – think about how you would do it differently if it happened again and then try this out if you have the opportunity.

Table 7.1 Example learning journal

Experience *significant event* *or incident*	*Last night was the first session with a new group and I felt it didn't go well. I focused too much on what I wanted to teach and too little on how and what the group wanted to learn.* *Some of the students stayed behind to ask a lot of questions that I thought I had addressed in the session, a few said they were confused and thought the programme would not meet their expectations.*
Describe *who, what,* *when, where*	*There were 16 students aged 29 to 65 attending an evening class (accountancy for beginners) from 6–9 p.m. The session took place in a classroom with a broken projector, windows that wouldn't open and not enough chairs.*
Analyse *why, how* *(impact on* *teaching and* *learning)*	*I should have arrived earlier to check that the projector was working as this delayed the session by 10 minutes. I had to move some chairs from the room across the corridor and leave the door wedged open to let fresh air in. Had I sorted this out prior to the students arriving, they would not have known of the problems. The class would then have started promptly and I would not have been flustered.* *I had too much paperwork to get through, the students had to fill in an enrolment form, I needed to carry out an initial assessment of their prior learning and ascertain if anyone had any particular needs. I also wanted them to take a learning styles test but there wasn't enough time. I had a list of things I wanted to get through, including an icebreaker and agreeing the ground rules but I forgot to agree the ground rules as I was rushing things. As a result I looked unprofessional.* *The icebreaker went well but was a bit hurried due to the late start. I had an induction checklist which kept me focused, but it was 7.30 p.m. before I realised the students needed a break. By this time, some of them were not paying attention to me but talking to others.* *I feel not a lot of learning took place as I was focusing too much on the paperwork and programme requirements.*
Revise *changes and/or* *improvements* *required*	*I will arrive earlier to ensure there are enough chairs and that the projector is working. I will apologise at the beginning of next week's session and I will ask what the students' expectations are and explain how I can meet them. We will set the ground rules next week.* *In future, I will interview all students in advance and ask them to complete the enrolment form, learning styles test and an initial assessment prior to their commencing. This will help me ascertain all the information I need to help plan my first session, and make it go more smoothly. It will also ensure they are all on the right programme. I have reported the windows to the caretaker. I will allow extra time in my session plan to account for questions and answers, and ensure the focus is upon their learning rather than my teaching.* *I have realised the first session is not about me and the paperwork I need to complete, but about what the students want to know and learn about the subject.*

Reflection should become a part of your everyday activities, enabling you to analyse and focus on things in greater detail. All reflection should lead to an improvement in practice; however, there may be events you would not want to change or improve as you felt they went well. If this is the case, reflect as to why they went well and use these methods in future sessions. If you are not able to write a reflective learning journal, mentally run through the EDAR points in your head when you have time. As you become more experienced at reflective practice, you will see how you can make improvements.

There are various theories regarding reflection. Schön (1983) suggests two methods:

- reflection in action
- reflection on action.

Reflection in action happens at the time of the incident, is often unconscious, is proactive and allows immediate changes to take place.

Example

Sarah was teaching a group of adults attending college as part of a day-release business studies programme. She had underestimated how fast they would learn as they were getting through the day's activities much more quickly than she had originally planned. At break time, she obtained some extra, more challenging, activities which she then used with the group. This enabled her to reflect immediately, ensuring the session was effective and meeting the students' needs. Sarah therefore carried out reflection in action.

Reflection on action takes place after the incident, is a more conscious process and is reactive. This allows you time to think about the incident, consider a different approach, or to talk to others about it before making changes.

Brookfield (1995) identified the importance of being critical when reflecting. He advocated four points of view when looking at practice which he called critical lenses. These lenses are from the point of view of:

- the teacher
- the student
- colleagues
- theories and literature.

Using these points makes the reflection critical, by firstly looking at it from your own point of view; secondly, how your student perceived your actions and what they liked and disliked; thirdly, the view from colleagues – for example, your mentor – is taken into consideration. This enables you to have a critical conversation about your actions which might highlight things you hadn't considered. Fourthly, you should link your reflections to theories and literature, comparing your own ideas with others.

The process of self-reflection and your own further development should help improve the quality of your delivery to your students.

Extension Activity

Reflect upon the next session you attend or teach. Evaluate how the session went, how you reacted to situations and what you would do differently next time. Research other reflective theorists such as Gibbs' (1988) reflective cycle.

Continuing professional development

There are constant changes in education; therefore it is crucial to keep up to date with any developments and new initiatives. Examples include changes to the qualifications you will teach, changes to policies and practices within your organisation, regulatory requirements and government policies. Your organisation may have a strategy for CPD which will prioritise activities they consider are important to improving standards. CPD can be formal or informal, planned well in advance or be opportunistic, but should have a real impact upon your teaching role, leading to an improvement in practice.

If you are working towards Associate or Qualified Teacher Status in the Learning and Skills Sector (ATLS/QTLS), you must evidence your CPD annually. Once you have achieved your ATLS or QTLS status, you will need to maintain your Licence to Practise by partaking in relevant CPD activities, which the IfL can monitor and sample.

Opportunities for professional development include:
- attending events and training programmes
- attending meetings
- e-learning activities
- evaluating feedback from peers and students
- improving own skills such as maths and English
- membership of professional associations or committees

- observing colleagues
- researching developments or changes to your subject and/or relevant legislation
- secondments
- self-reflection
- shadowing colleagues
- standardisation activities
- studying for relevant qualifications
- subscribing to and reading relevant journals and websites
- visiting other organisations
- voluntary work
- work experience placements
- writing or reviewing books and articles.

All CPD activities must be documented in some way and reflected upon. This can be via the IfL website, your organisation's systems, or your own manual or electronic record. Maintaining your CPD will ensure you are not only competent at your job role, but also up to date with the latest developments regarding your specialist subject and teaching and learning approaches.

The following websites are useful to gain up-to-date information regarding developments in the Lifelong Learning Sector.

Department for Business, Innovation and Skills – www.bis.gov.uk

Department for Education – www.education.gov.uk

Equality and Diversity Forum – www.edf.org.uk

Government updates: Education and Learning –
www.direct.gov.uk/en/EducationAndLearning/index.htm

Institute for Learning – www.ifl.ac.uk

Learning and Skills Improvement Service – www.lsis.org.uk

National Institute of Adult Continuing Education – www.niace.org.uk

Ofqual – www.ofqual.gov.uk/

Times Educational Supplement Online – www.tes.co.uk

Extension Activity

Thinking about the subject you wish to teach, what do you need to do to ensure you are up to date and current with your knowledge and skills? Access the websites listed above and subscribe to any regular electronic updates.

Progression

Before you complete your PTLLS Award, you may find it useful to summarise your learning and create an action plan or summative profile for your future development. This could be a list of your strengths and achievements so far, areas you would like to develop or improve, and how you will work towards accomplishing them. All teachers must register with the IfL within six months of starting their job role and gain the PTLLS Award within one year. PTLLS holders will be classed as an Affiliate member until fully qualified. Membership of the IfL does not give you your teaching status; a separate process must be gone through to achieve your Licence to Practise (ATLS or QTLS, depending on your job role).

After achieving the PTLLS Award, you should work towards a higher-level teaching qualification which will depend upon your job role as either an Associate or Full teacher (see Chapter 1). An Associate teacher does not carry out or have the responsibilities that a Full teacher would, i.e. they might teach programmes where someone else has designed the scheme of work, session plans and resources. Associate teachers must take the CTLLS. Full teachers must take the DTTLS, also known as the Certificate in Education or Post Graduate/Professional Certificate in Education (PGCE).

You will also need to demonstrate you have achieved the minimum core skills of literacy, language, numeracy and ICT.

Once you have achieved the required qualifications, you will undertake an induction period, known as Professional Formation. This is:

> . . . the post-qualification process by which a teacher demonstrates through professional practice:
>
> 1. the ability to use effectively the skills and knowledge acquired whilst train-ing to be a teacher;
>
> 2. and the capacity to meet the occupational standards required of a teacher.
> (The Further Education Teachers' Qualifications (England) Regulations, 2007)

Once you have successfully achieved the required teaching qualifications and minimum core skills, and completed the professional formation process, you can apply to the IfL for your teaching status and Licence to Practise. The teaching status of ATLS is for Associate teachers. QTLS is for Full teachers and does not relate to whether you are employed part time or full time.

Register with the IfL online at www.ifl.ac.uk. You will need to have details of your teaching and specialist subject qualifications available. (This would be a good time to update your curriculum vitae and CPD record.) Have a look at the different pages on the IfL website to familiarise yourself with the process of how to gain your Licence to Practise.

Summary

In this chapter you have learnt about:

- quality assurance
- evaluation
- self-reflection and learning journals
- Continuing Professional Development
- progression.

Cross-referencing grid

This chapter contributes towards the following: scope (S), knowledge (K) and practice (P) aspects of the Professional Teaching Standards (A–F domains) and the PTLLS units' assessment criteria. Full details of the learning outcomes and assessment criteria for each PTLLS unit can be found in the appendices.

Domain	Standards
A	AS4, AS7, AK4.2, AK4.3, AK7.2, AK7.3, AP4.2, AP4.3, AP7.2, AP7.3
B	BS2, BK2.6, BP2.6, BP2.7
C	CSI, CS3, CS4, CKI.I, CK3.4, CK4.I, CPI.I, CP3.3, CP3.4, CP4.I
D	DS3, DK3.I, DK3.2, DP2.I, DP3.2
E	ES4, EK4.2, EK5.I, EP4.2, EP5.I
F	FS3, FP3.I

PTLLS unit	Assessment criteria	
	Level 3	Level 4
Roles, responsibilities and relationships in lifelong learning		
Understanding inclusive learning and teaching in lifelong learning		
Using inclusive learning and teaching approaches in lifelong learning	2.I 3.I 3.2	2.I 3.I 3.2
Principles of assessment in lifelong learning		

Theory focus

References and further information

Brookfield, SD (1995) *Becoming a Critically Reflective Teacher.* San Francisco: Jossey Bass.

Gibbs, G (1988) *Learning by Doing: A guide to teaching and learning methods.* Oxford: Further Education Unit.

Gravells, A (2012) *Achieving your TAQA Assessor and Internal Quality Assurer Award.* Exeter: Learning Matters.

Gravells, A and Simpson, S (2010) *Planning and Enabling Learning in the Lifelong Learning Sector* (2nd edn). Exeter: Learning Matters.

Schön, D (1983) *The Reflective Practitioner.* London: Temple Smith.

The Further Education Teachers' Qualifications (England) Regulations (2007) SI 2007/2264. London: HMSO. Available at: www.legislation.gov.uk/uksi/2007/2264/pdfs/uksi20072264_en.pdf (accessed October 2011).

Wallace, S (2011) *Achieving QTLS: Teaching, tutoring and training in the Lifelong Learning Sector* (4th edn). Exeter: Learning Matters.

Wood, J and Dickinson, J (2011) *Quality Assurance and Evaluation in the Lifelong Learning Sector.* Exeter: Learning Matters.

Websites

English and Maths online learning – www.move-on.org.uk

Institute for Learning (IfL) – www.ifl.ac.uk

Minimum Core shortcut – http://tinyurl.com/3l5rhvl

Introduction

> In this chapter you will learn about:
>
> - planning
> - preparing
> - delivering
> - evaluating

This chapter will assist you in preparation for your micro-teach session. At the end of each section is an activity to help you to put theory into practice. Guidance is given for pre-service and in-service micro-teach sessions. A more detailed version of this chapter appears in *Passing PTLLS Assessments* by Ann Gravells.

At the end of the chapter is a cross-referencing grid showing how the chapter's contents contribute towards the professional teaching standards and PTLLS units.

Planning

To achieve the PTLLS Award you need to demonstrate your skills and knowledge as a teacher. You are therefore required to plan, prepare, deliver and evaluate a short teaching session. This will be either to your peers if you are pre-service or to your current students if you are in-service. This gives you the opportunity to put theory into practice and will usually be for a minimum of 15 or 30 minutes, the date, time and place being agreed in advance. You will be assessed by your teacher or an observer who will probably use an observation checklist, which you would find useful to see in advance. This will help you know what they are looking for and enable you to ask any questions beforehand. Your observer might make a visual recording of your session which you can view to help your evaluation process. This will enable you to see things you were not aware of: for example, saying *erm*, using a lot of hand gestures or not using enough eye contact with your students. You should be told in advance if you are going to be recorded; try not to be put off by it, but embrace it as a way of developing yourself further.

You may find it useful to ask your observer the following questions.

- How long will my session be?
- When and where will it take place?
- Will you need to see my session plan in advance?
- What if I change my mind about what I'm going to do?
- What equipment and resources are available to me?
- How many people will I be delivering to?
- Do I need to know their learning styles or any individual needs?
- Can I find out in advance what prior knowledge and/or experience my students have of my subject?
- Can I show a vieo clip? If so, how long can it be?
- What will I need to bring with me, e.g. board markers, clock, paper?
- Can I arrive early to set up the area, e.g. move tables, check resources?
- What computer programs/versions are available?
- Will I have internet access?
- Should I e-mail my presentation to you or should I bring it on a memory stick?
- Is there somewhere I can get handouts photocopied in advance?
- Should I start with an icebreaker and ground rules?
- What kind of assessment activity should I use?
- How will I receive feedback afterwards?

You will need to create a session plan in advance which should have a clear aim (what you want your students to achieve), which is then broken down into objectives (how your students will achieve your aim). Your plan should show what you expect your students to achieve expressed in a way that will enable you to assess that learning has taken place. Your observer will probably want to see your session plan well in advance to give you advice and support. See Chapter 4 for guidance regarding session planning.

Your session plan should have a beginning (the introduction), a middle section (the development) and an ending (the summary/conclusion) which should show a logical progression of learning and assessment. Timings should be allocated to each of the teaching and learning activities you plan to use in each section.

Activity

Obtain the session plan pro-forma you are required to use for your micro-teach session and complete it with the relevant details. Decide upon your aim, objectives, and the teaching, learning and assessment activities you will use. Allocate timings to each of these activities – for example, five minutes, ten minutes, etc. – to ensure you can cover everything within the allocated time.

Think of a few questions you need to ask your observer and ensure that you obtain the answers before your micro-teach session.

Preparing

Once you have your session plan, you will need to design all the activities, hand-outs, resources, presentations and assessment activities you intend to use. You may need to learn how to use something in advance: for example, if you wish to use a computerised presentation during your session. You should check all presentations and handouts for spelling, grammar and punctuation errors and ensure text and pictures represent all aspects of equality and diversity. If you are delivering a 30-minute session and you plan to show a video for ten minutes, this will not demonstrate how teaching and learning are taking place. Videos are good for visual students, but if used, keep them short or you may lose the attention of other students.

Carry out a trial run with friends or family to check your timings. You might find that what you planned to cover in 30 minutes takes only 20. Time will go quickly during your micro-teach session, particularly if you are asked lots of questions. Make sure you have all the necessary equipment, resources and stationery. A clock or a watch in a visible place will help you keep track of time. Try to have a contingency plan in case anything goes wrong: for example, a hard copy of an electronic presentation.

If possible check in advance and/or arrive early to see that everything is available and working in the room you will be in. You may want to rearrange the area beforehand to suit your subject and to enable everyone to see and hear you. Time for setting up and clearing away afterwards should be outside of your observed time. You may need two copies of your session plan, one for yourself and one for your observer.

Activity

Rehearse your micro-teach session to a few trusted people. Make sure you have your session plan and all relevant resources to hand. Although this is a role-play activity, treat it seriously and work through all your planned teaching, learning and assessment activities. Afterwards, ask for feedback as to how you could improve your session. You might have to revise your session plan timings or redesign some resources as a result.

Delivering

The micro-teach is a learning experience and a chance to put all your new-found theory into practice. You may feel nervous as you will be observed. However, try to imagine you are playing a role and this should help your confidence. You are the teacher in this situation; you need to be in control and not let any personal issues affect you. If you are organised and have checked the room and equipment in advance, hopefully you won't encounter any problems. Try to relax, but stay focused and above all enjoy yourself. As you will have prepared your session plan carefully, your delivery should follow logically through the introduction, development and summary stages.

Introduction

Before you speak, take a few deep breaths, smile at your students and use eye contact; this should help you to relax. Begin by saying *Hello, my name is …*, followed by your aim and objectives. You might like to keep these on display throughout your session — perhaps on a piece of flipchart paper on the wall. Don't tell your students that you are nervous as it probably won't show. Stand tall and speak a little more loudly and slowly than normal as being anxious or nervous may make you speak more quickly. If you feel you are shaking, it is highly likely no one will notice. If your mind suddenly goes blank, take a couple of deep breaths for a few seconds and look at your session plan to help you refocus; it might seem a long time to you but it won't to your students. You will need to establish a rapport with your students and engage and interact with them from the start. Asking the question *Has anyone done this before?* is a good way of involving your students in your subject from the start and helps you check any prior learning.

Keep your session plan handy as a prompt. If you feel you might forget something, use a highlight pen beforehand to mark key words which you can quickly look at. Use eye contact with all your students and standing rather than sitting will help your confidence and voice projection. Keep things simple, don't try to deliver too much material, or expect too much from your students — your subject may be very new to them. If this is the first time you have met your students, you might want to carry out a short icebreaker with them or ask them to introduce themselves to you. You may not have time to agree any ground rules; however, you could state that you expect mobile phones to be switched off. You might like to encourage your students to ask questions if they need to clarify any points.

Development

You should use a variety of teaching and learning approaches to reach all learning styles and to retain motivation. Summarise and recap regularly to reinforce points, and ask open questions to check knowledge. Try to use names when talking to your students and if possible address everyone in the group; don't just focus on a particular student who you know can give you the correct answers. Having your students' names written down in advance will help. Try to use the PPP (Pose, Pause, Pounce) method when asking questions.

The timing of activities needs to be followed carefully; if you are only delivering a 15-minute session you may not have time for group activities. If you do set activities, think what you will be doing while your students are working: i.e. moving around the room and observing or asking questions shows you are in control. Longer sessions benefit from a mixture of teaching and learning approaches to ensure all learning styles will be met.

Summary/Conclusion

A short quiz or multiple-choice test towards the end of your session is a good way to check knowledge if you have time, and acts as an assessment activity. Your summary should recap your aim and objectives. You might like to ask your students if they have any questions. However, you may be met with silence, or they might have lots of questions which will then eat into your time. If you find you have covered everything and have spare time, you could ask each member of the group to state one thing they feel they have learnt from the session. This is a good way of filling in spare time if necessary, and shows you what each student has learnt. You could prepare a handout in advance which summarises your session and this could be given at the end. If you issue it during the session your students will look at it and not you.

If you are unsure of how to end your session, simply say *Thank you*; this will indicate to your group you have finished. Make sure you leave the area tidy afterwards.

Pre-service micro-teach session

As a pre-service teacher you will be delivering to a group of your peers who will become your students for the session. This might be the first time you have taught a group of people and your peers will probably be very encouraging and supportive. If you have chosen to deliver a subject you know well, your knowledge should help your confidence. You will probably be in the same environment you have been learning in, or a central meeting point if you have been studying through a distance-learning programme. Hopefully you will have met your peers previously and feel comfortable delivering to them; if not, it would be useful to talk to them beforehand to help everyone relax. If you are due to deliver after someone else, you will probably be thinking about your own micro-teach session rather than focusing upon theirs. Try not to do this as it may make you more nervous. Being well prepared and having self-confidence and knowledge of your subject should help alleviate any worries.

In-service teaching session

You might be required to deliver your session to your peers rather than to your own students. If this is the case, please read the pre-service section above. However, delivering to your peer group would be a good time to try out something different or new in a safe environment, rather than repeating a session you would normally deliver to your own students.

You might already have some experience of teaching, therefore delivering a session to your own students should be fairly straightforward. Your session might last longer than the time your observer will be present; they might therefore miss the beginning or ending and arrive part way through. You should try to plan the session to allow time to talk to your observer either before or afterwards. This will enable you to discuss your delivery, justify any aspects they have missed and to receive feedback. The session you are delivering may be one of many, for which you will have a scheme of work to follow. You may want to introduce the observer to the group and state they are observing you, not them. Having a stranger in the room might lead to some behaviour issues. If so, you must deal with these as soon as they arise and in a professional manner.

Activity

Imagine the group you will deliver your micro-teach session to is made up of the following: six females and eight males aged between 16 and 65, from a variety of backgrounds. Three are unemployed, one is dyslexic and one is a wheelchair user. Learning styles are: nine kinaesthetic, two visual, two read/write and one aural. What adaptations would you make to your session plan to ensure you differentiate for individual needs and include everyone in the session?

Evaluating

After your delivery you may find that your observer asks you how you felt it went before giving feedback. This will enable you to consider what went well and what you could have done differently. You should receive oral feedback along with a completed observation checklist. You might also receive feedback from your peers which can be used to inform your self-evaluation process. Once you have finished your micro-teach session, you might be so relieved or busy packing away that you don't fully take on board what is being said to you.

Listen carefully and ask questions to clarify any points you are unsure of. Try not to interrupt or become defensive when receiving feedback and don't take anything personally – the feedback will be given to help you improve.

Evaluating your delivery is an important aspect of your learning and development and you may need to complete a self-evaluation form to formalise this. You might think you have done really well, but you may have received some helpful advice during the feedback process which could help you improve further.

When evaluating yourself, consider your strengths, areas for development and any action and improvements required from a teaching perspective as well as a subject perspective. Hopefully, you enjoyed your micro-teach session and it has confirmed you do want to have a career as a teacher. However, the experience might have made you think that teaching just isn't for you at this point in time. Conversely it might make you more determined to improve and develop further.

Activity

After you have delivered your role-play micro-teach and received feedback, evaluate your strengths and areas for development. Did you achieve your aim effectively? Did your students achieve the objectives? Analyse the effectiveness of the resources you used and consider what you would change or modify for your actual micro-teach session.

Summary

In this chapter you have learnt about:

- planning
- preparing
- delivering
- evaluating.

Cross-referencing grid

This chapter contributes towards the following: scope (S), knowledge (K) and practice (P) aspects of the Professional Teaching Standards (A–F domains) and the PTLLS units' assessment criteria. Full details of the learning outcomes and assessment criteria for each PTLLS unit can be found in the appendices.

Domain	Standards
A	ASI, AS4, AS7, AK7.3, API.I, AP4.I, AP4.2, AP6.2, AP7.3
B	BSI, BS2, BS3, BS5, BK2.6, BK3.I, BK3.2, BK3.3, BPI.I, BPI.2, BPI.3, BP2.I, BP2.2, BP2.3, BP2.4, BP2.6, BP3.I, BP3.2, BP3.3, BP3.4, BP5.I, BP5.2
C	CS2, CS4, CKI.I, CK2.I, CP2.I, CP3.I
D	DSI, DS3, DKI.I, DKI.2, DKI.3, DK2.I, DK3.I, DPI.I, DPI.2, DPI.3, DP2.I, DP3.I
E	ESI, ES2, ES4, EKI.I, EKI.2, EKI.3, EK2.3, EK4.2, EPI.I, EPI.2, EPI.3, EP2.I, EP2.2, EP2.3, EP4.I, EP4.2
F	

PTLLS unit	Assessment criteria	
	Level 3	Level 4
Roles, responsibilities and relationships in lifelong learning		
Understanding inclusive learning and teaching in lifelong learning		
Using inclusive learning and teaching approaches in lifelong learning	3.I, 3.2	3.I, 3.2
Principles of assessment in lifelong learning	2.2	2.2

Theory focus

References and further information

Duckworth, V, Wood, J, Bostock, J and Dickinson, J (2010) *Successful Teaching Practice in the Lifelong Learning Sector.* Exeter: Learning Matters.

Gravells, A (2010) *Passing PTLLS Assessments.* Exeter: Learning Matters.

Websites

Oxford Learning Institute – Giving and receiving feedback – http://tinyurl.com/688tfev

Unit title: Roles, responsibilities and relationships in lifelong learning
Level 3 (3 credits)

Learning outcomes The learner will:	Assessment criteria The learner can:
1. Understand own role and responsibilities in lifelong learning	1.1 Summarise key aspects of legislation, regulatory requirements and codes of practice relating to own role and responsibilities
	1.2 Explain own responsibilities for equality and valuing diversity
	1.3 Explain own role and responsibilities in lifelong learning
	1.4 Explain own role and responsibilities in identifying and meeting the needs of learners
2. Understand the relationships between teachers and other professionals in lifelong learning	2.1 Explain the boundaries between the teaching role and other professional roles
	2.2 Describe points of referral to meet the needs of learners
	2.3 Summarise own responsibilities in relation to other professionals
3. Understand own responsibility for maintaining a safe and supportive learning environment	3.1 Explain own responsibilities in maintaining a safe and supportive learning environment
	3.2 Explain how to promote appropriate behaviour and respect for others

**Unit title: Roles, responsibilities and relationships in lifelong learning
Level 4 (3 credits)**

Learning outcomes The learner will:	Assessment criteria The learner can:
1. Understand own role and responsibilities in lifelong learning	1.1 Summarise key aspects of legislation, regulatory requirements and codes of practice relating to own role and responsibilities
	1.2 Analyse own responsibilities for promoting equality and valuing diversity
	1.3 Evaluate own role and responsibilities in lifelong learning
	1.4 Review own role and responsibilities in identifying and meeting the needs of learners
2. Understand the relationships between teachers and other professionals in lifelong learning	2.1 Analyse the boundaries between the teaching role and other professional roles
	2.2 Review points of referral to meet the needs of learners
	2.3 Evaluate own responsibilities in relation to other professionals
3. Understand own responsibility for maintaining a safe and supportive learning environment	3.1 Explain how to establish and maintain a safe and supportive learning environment
	3.2 Explain how to promote appropriate behaviour and respect for others

Unit title: Understanding inclusive learning and teaching in lifelong learning
Level 3 (3 credits)

Learning outcomes The learner will:	Assessment criteria The learner can:
1. Understand learning and teaching strategies in lifelong learning	1.1 Summarise learning and teaching strategies used in own specialism
	1.2 Explain how approaches to learning and teaching in own specialism meet the needs of learners
	1.3 Describe aspects of inclusive learning
2. Understand how to create inclusive learning and teaching in lifelong learning	2.1 Explain how to select inclusive learning and teaching techniques
	2.2 Explain how to select resources that meet the needs of learners
	2.3 Explain how to create assessment opportunities that meet the needs of learners
	2.4 Explain how to provide opportunities for learners to practise their literacy, language, numeracy and ICT skills
3. Understand ways to create a motivating learning environment	3.1 Explain ways to engage and motivate learners in an inclusive learning environment
	3.2 Summarise ways to establish ground rules with learners to promote respect for others
	3.3 Explain ways to give constructive feedback that motivates learners

Unit title: Understanding inclusive learning and teaching in lifelong learning
Level 4 (3 credits)

Learning outcomes The learner will:	Assessment criteria The learner can:
1. Understand learning and teaching strategies in lifelong learning	1.1 Analyse learning and teaching strategies used in own specialism
	1.2 Evaluate the effectiveness of approaches to learning and teaching in own specialist area in meeting needs of learners
	1.3 Evaluate aspects of inclusive learning
2. Understand how to create inclusive learning and teaching in lifelong learning	2.1 Analyse inclusive approaches to learning and teaching
	2.2 Analyse how to select resources to meet the needs of learners
	2.3 Explain how to create assessment opportunities that meet the needs of learners
	2.4 Review how to provide opportunities for learners to practise their literacy, language, numeracy and ICT skills
3. Understand how to create a motivating learning environment	3.1 Explain how to engage and motivate learners in an inclusive learning environment
	3.2 Explain how to establish ground rules with learners to promote respect for others
	3.3 Review ways to give constructive feedback to motivate learners

Unit title: Using inclusive learning and teaching approaches in lifelong learning
Level 3 (3 credits)

Learning outcomes The learner will:	Assessment criteria The learner can:
1. Be able to plan inclusive learning and teaching sessions	1.1 Plan a session for learning and teaching that meets the needs of learners
	1.2 Justify the selection of approaches to meet the needs of learners
	1.3 Plan assessment methods to meet the needs of learners
2. Be able to deliver inclusive learning and teaching sessions	2.1 Apply learning and teaching approaches to meet the needs of learners
	2.2 Use resources to meet the needs of learners
	2.3 Communicate with learners to meet their needs and aid their understanding
	2.4 Provide constructive feedback to learners
3. Be able to evaluate own practice in delivering inclusive learning and teaching	3.1 Reflect on own approaches to delivering inclusive learning and teaching
	3.2 Identify areas for improvement in own practice

Unit title: Using inclusive learning and teaching approaches in lifelong learning
Level 4 (3 credits)

Learning outcomes The learner will:	Assessment criteria The learner can:
1. Be able to plan inclusive learning and teaching sessions	1.1 Plan a session for learning and teaching that meets the needs of learners
	1.2 Justify the selection of approaches to meet the needs of learners
2. Be able to deliver inclusive learning and teaching sessions	2.1 Demonstrate inclusive learning and teaching approaches to engage and motivate learners
	2.2 Demonstrate the use of appropriate resources to support inclusive learning and teaching
	2.3 Use assessment methods to support learning and teaching
	2.4 Communicate with learners to meet their needs and aid their understanding
	2.5 Provide constructive feedback to learners
3. Be able to evaluate own practice in delivering inclusive learning and teaching	3.1 Review own approaches to delivering inclusive learning and teaching
	3.2 Analyse how own inclusive learning and teaching practice can be improved to meet the needs of learners

Unit title: Principles of assessment in lifelong learning
Level 3 (3 credits)

Learning outcomes The learner will:	Assessment criteria The learner can:
1. Understand types and methods of assessment used in lifelong learning	1.1 Explain types of assessment used in lifelong learning
	1.2 Explain the use of methods of assessment in lifelong learning
	1.3 Compare the strengths and limitations of assessment methods to meet individual learner needs
2. Understand ways to involve learners in the assessment process	2.1 Explain ways to involve the learner in the assessment process
	2.2 Explain the role of peer and self-assessment in the assessment process
3. Understand requirements for keeping records of assessment in lifelong learning	3.1 Explain the need to keep records of assessment of learning
	3.2 Summarise the requirements for keeping records of assessment in an organisation

Unit title: Principles of assessment in lifelong learning
Level 4 (3 credits)

Learning outcomes The learner will:	Assessment criteria The learner can:
1. Understand how types and methods of assessment are used in lifelong learning	1.1 Analyse how types of assessment are used in lifelong learning
	1.2 Analyse how assessment methods are used in lifelong learning
	1.3 Evaluate strengths and limitations of assessment methods to meet individual learner needs
2. Understand how to involve learners in the assessment process	2.1 Evaluate how to involve the learner in the assessment process
	2.2 Analyse the role of peer and self-assessment in the assessment process
3. Understand requirements for keeping records of assessment in lifelong learning	3.1 Explain the need to keep records of assessment of learning
	3.2 Summarise the requirements for keeping records of assessment in an organisation

Teaching and learning checklist
Identifying needs
Do I...?

- ☐ Know who I will be teaching, i.e. details of all students and any specific requirements
- ☐ Know anything about the students that might affect my teaching or their learning
- ☐ Need to carry out an initial assessment or diagnostic test with students
- ☐ Need to carry out a learning styles test with students
- ☐ Need to agree an action plan or individual learning plan with students
- ☐ Need to learn anything myself before I can teach the subject
- ☐ Know the organisational policies such as health and safety, equality and diversity, safeguarding, etc., and carry out any risk assessments or necessary checks

Planning learning
Do I...?

- ☐ Have a syllabus or qualification handbook
- ☐ Have an induction checklist
- ☐ Need to create a scheme of work which shows a logical progression of learning
- ☐ Need to create a session plan
- ☐ Have clear aims and SMART objectives
- ☐ Know when and where I will be teaching, to how many and for how long
- ☐ Need to prepare the learning environment
- ☐ Need a clock or watch to keep track of time
- ☐ Need to book or obtain any specialist equipment or resources
- ☐ Need to know any organisational procedures, e.g. fire exits, accidents, appeals
- ☐ Need to find out where facilities are, such as toilets, refreshments
- ☐ Need to arrange refreshments, transport or parking
- ☐ Need to send out any pre-programme information and/or inform reception staff where to direct students
- ☐ Need to devise suitable learning activities, resources and assessments and get these photocopied or uploaded to a VLE
- ☐ Need to check spelling, grammar and punctuation of presentations and handouts
- ☐ Have a contingency plan in case anything goes wrong, and extra activities if needed

Facilitating learning
Can I...?

- ☐ Ensure the environment is suitable, e.g. heating, lighting, ventilation, seating arrangements and disability access
- ☐ Arrive early to set up and check equipment, obtain resources, etc.
- ☐ Complete any necessary administrative requirements, e.g. register
- ☐ Introduce the session aims and objectives (or learning outcomes)
- ☐ Recap the previous session (if applicable)
- ☐ Use an icebreaker, energiser or starter activity
- ☐ Negotiate ground rules
- ☐ Stipulate the times of breaks
- ☐ Use a variety of teaching and learning approaches, activities and resources to include and differentiate for all students, taking into account equality and diversity
- ☐ Mix formal and informal teaching in an appropriate manner
- ☐ Manage behaviour and disruption as it occurs
- ☐ Take any additional student needs into consideration and support students as necessary
- ☐ Use student names and ask individual questions
- ☐ Leave personal problems behind and act professionally at all times
- ☐ Prepare an extension activity for students who finish tasks earlier than others, or need challenging further
- ☐ Allow time for questions
- ☐ Summarise the session and recap aims and objectives (or learning outcomes)
- ☐ Leave the venue tidy
- ☐ Maintain all relevant records

Assessing learning
Can I...?

- ☐ Ensure the validity and reliability of all assessment methods
- ☐ Ask open questions to check knowledge
- ☐ Assess students on an individual basis – formally and informally
- ☐ Give feedback to students on an individual basis in a constructive manner
- ☐ Review student progress, e.g. through tutorials
- ☐ Keep records of progress and assessment decisions

Quality assurance and Evaluation
Did I...?

- ☐ Deliver an introduction, main content and summary
- ☐ Follow the timings on the session plan; if not, what would I change and why
- ☐ Establish and maintain a rapport, putting students at ease
- ☐ Project energy, enthusiasm and passion for the subject

- [ ] Have a structured approach
- [ ] Remain in control and deal with any difficult or unexpected situations appropriately
- [ ] Appear confident and professional with a positive attitude
- [ ] Use eye contact with all students
- [ ] Use individual names
- [ ] Fidget or fiddle with anything; if so, how could I stop
- [ ] Listen actively
- [ ] Dress and act appropriately
- [ ] Answer questions appropriately
- [ ] Recap key points regularly
- [ ] Use appropriate body language and non-verbal communication
- [ ] Limit the use of jargon or acronyms
- [ ] Achieve the aim enabling the students to achieve their objectives (or learning outcomes)
- [ ] Provide opportunities for student feedback
- [ ] Enjoy the session; if not, why not
- [ ] Follow all regulations and codes of practice
- [ ] Reflect on the session content, along with the teaching and learning process to make improvements for the future

INDEX